SHAPES AND NAMES
OF
ATHENIAN VASES

The Metropolitan Museum of Art

SHAPES AND NAMES
OF
ATHENIAN VASES

By

GISELA M. A. RICHTER, LITT. D., L.H.D.

AND

MARJORIE J. MILNE, PH.D.

McGrath Publishing Company

WASHINGTON, D.C.

1973

Τὸ μὲν δὴ κάλλος ἐν τῇ τῶν μορίων συμμετρίᾳ ἐστίν.

Beauty consists in the proportionate distribution of parts.

CHRYSIPPOS

PREFACE

THE pamphlet SHAPES OF GREEK VASES, published in 1922, was written primarily for potters. Its appeal, however, proved to be wider, and it was extensively used as a picture book by archae-ologists. The present book, SHAPES AND NAMES OF ATHENIAN VASES, has therefore been designed to serve a larger public. The interest and the potential popularity of the subject, as well as the lack of a recent, up-to-date treatment of it, seemed to justify a more extended study. Instead of merely showing the chief shapes in a few examples, we have tried to trace the development of each form from period to period, utilizing as far as possible the material in this Museum. Only when an important type is missing here, and there would have been a conspicuous gap in the series, have we included specimens from other collections. (Unless otherwise stated the vases illustrated are in this Museum.) We have also added to most sections a picture illustrating the use of the shape and a discussion of its probable ancient name. Since it is helpful to call the various shapes by specific names, ancient ones have been generally adopted by archaeologists, some identified on good grounds, others used merely for convenience. We thought it of interest carefully to sift this evidence, which is often extraordi-narily confused. A selected bibliography has been included.

Miss Milne is chiefly responsible for the sections dealing with the ancient names of vases, Miss Richter for the rest of the text and for the selection of the illustrations. Our debt to J. D. Beazley is evident from the frequent citations of his works in the bibliog-raphy; and we have also had the benefit of his reading of the manuscript.

GISELA M. A. RICHTER

MARJORIE J. MILNE

TABLE OF CONTENTS

INTRODUCTION

THE sense of harmonious composition which was characteristic of the Greek people is well illustrated in their pottery. These vases—the jars, dishes, and cups made for household use—were designed with intelligent skill to serve their purpose effectively; but by the beauty of their shapes no less than by their decoration they rank as works of art.

Compared with the vases of other countries, which are designed mostly in continuous curves, Greek pottery is strongly articulated. The various parts—mouth, neck, body, foot—are generally set off from one another, lip and foot are often in several degrees, and handles are usually added. The harmonious proportions of these parts give to a Greek pot the distinctive character of a well-designed structure. In the shapes the influence of contemporary metalware can often be detected; and sometimes even such details as handle attachments and heads of rivets are copied in clay (cf. figs. 68, 123). But always the difference of material is taken into account and the precise metal shapes are translated into rounded, plastic forms.

The shapes illustrated in this book have been selected from Athenian vases of the sixth to the fourth century B.C. Naturally each form both had a previous history and persisted after this period; for the same continuity may be traced in Greek pottery as in Greek sculpture. But during these two centuries or so in Attica—particularly in the late sixth and the early fifth— the Greek sense for form finds perhaps its happiest expression.

Athenian black- and red-figured pottery was all made of red clay, decorated with black glaze, and low-fired (about 960° centigrade). Except for the comparatively few vases molded in the forms of heads, figures, etc., it was wheel-thrown and turned, that is, the pieces were formed on the wheel and afterwards refined with metal tools. Each pot therefore was an individual creation. There were no table services with dozens of identical dishes, no mass production in factories. But neither was there an endless number of forms. For the Greek potter was content to adhere to a few prescribed shapes and to repeat these again and again with only subtle changes in details. Like the early Greek sculptor he made his individual contribution within an accepted scheme. New inventions were rare; instead there was a constant, slow growth, a development of a type into specific forms expressive of their time. Gradually the sturdy shapes of the early sixth century became refined into the harmonious forms of the late sixth and early fifth century; then became slighter, more elongated, more graceful; and finally disintegrated into the weaker products of the fourth century. But if we compare several contemporary examples of a certain shape we realize how strictly a given scheme was followed. Not only do they correspond in a general way but the same forms of lips, feet, handles, shoulders are repeated again and again. A shape once evolved was evidently felt to be satisfying. And yet there is no monotony in this repetition; for within the prescribed limits there is constant variation in size, curves, proportion.

To modern artists this self-imposed restriction by a highly original people comes as a surprise, but also as a revelation. For to this amazing concentration is largely due the satisfying quality of Athenian vases. They are not the product of a sudden inspiration but the result of a continued, united effort. Their carefully thought-out forms and proportions partake of the permanence of architecture. To become intimately acquainted with these Greek forms, to appreciate their subtle distinctions, to watch the slow development from decade to decade is to obtain an insight into the Greek mind and also to train our own artistic perceptions.

Athenian vases are not only finely proportioned, they are also well adapted for their various uses. The round or trefoil mouths of the wine jugs (cf. figs. 114–134) are so formed that the liquids can be poured without spilling. Through the narrow necks of the oil and perfume jugs (cf. figs. 91–111) the fluid flows drop by drop or in a thin stream, while their bowl-like mouths are convenient funnels for filling. The danger of dripping after pouring is obviated by the sharp incline of the inside of the mouth or by a channel to catch the liquid or by an unglazed portion which tends to absorb the drops and so arrest them. Contrary, perhaps, to expectation the kylix (cf. figs. 152 ff.) is a convenient drinking cup, for the slight convex curve on the inside of the rim prevents the liquid from spilling down one's cheeks. The wide-mouthed mixing bowls are admirably adapted for having liquids poured into them or ladled out of them. The tall water jars with their broad bowls and fairly narrow necks are well designed for being carried from the fountain without spilling the contents. The feet—especially of large vases—are substantial, with a broad, unglazed band for the vase to rest on and with the interior hollowed out (cf. fig. 157). The lids[1] fit well, generally with plenty of leeway, and are set on substantial ledges.

[1] Lids were much commoner than the many now lidless vases would lead one to suppose. The amphora, stamnos, and lebes gamikos were regularly provided with lids.

The handles form an especially interesting study. Their shapes, their sizes, their positions on the vase are nicely calculated for convenient holding or lifting or inserting a crooked finger (cf. figs. 76 ff.). And they seem to grow out of the body like the branches of a tree, a slight swelling at the juncture forming a pleasing transition and adding to the solidity. When a handle of a Greek vase breaks off it usually carries part of the body with it. The ridges often observable at the junctures of neck and body or of body and foot form attractive accents and sometimes have a practical purpose. For Athenian vases, at least those of large dimensions, were made in sections; the junctures of these sections were conveniently placed at the articulations of the vase where the ridges would serve still further to hide the joints (cf. fig. 57).

The ancient names of Greek vases present a difficult problem. With a limited number of shapes made for special uses during several centuries it would seem natural that each vase should be given a specific name in addition to its general designation as a jar, bowl, jug, or cup. As a matter of fact a large number of such names current in antiquity are known both from incidental allusions by authors contemporary with the vases and from lists and descriptions in late writers. Sometimes, by a lucky chance, an inscription naming a vase appears either on the pot itself or in a scene where it is represented (cf. pp. 11, 14, 24). Furthermore, in the scenes on Greek vases are frequent representations of pots in actual use—which help in judging the descriptions of them.

With such explicit evidence one would expect that the identification of the ancient names of the vases would be a comparatively easy matter. But this is not the case. Archaeologists have long struggled with the problem. As long ago as 1829 Panofka published a book entitled *Recherches sur les véritables noms des vases grecs et sur leurs différens usages d'après les témoignages des auteurs et des monumens anciens*. His optimistic conclusion that he had reëstablished the ancient nomenclature was soon challenged by Gerhard[2] and especially by Letronne.[3] Jahn in his catalogue of the Greek vases in Munich, published in 1854, summed up in a scientific manner the conclusions obtainable in his day. Since then various writers have at times utilized occasional scraps of new evidence furnished by later discoveries.

The great difficulty, of course, lies in the facts that our information is largely derived from late writers—Athenaios, Pollux, other lexicographers, and the scholiasts—who tried to explain forms often unknown to them and so gave contradictory descriptions, and that different names for the same shape were apparently current at different times and in different places. It

[2] *Annali dell' Instituto di corrispondenza archeologica*, 1831, vol. III, pp. 221 ff.
[3] *Observations . . . sur les noms des vases grecs.*

must also be remembered that a generic name like water jar or cup may be applied to different forms, each of which can have a specific name. Thus hydria must be the right name to apply to the three-handled jar often represented as a water jar on Greek vases; but it could also be used to designate an amphora or any other vessel filled with water (cf. p. 12).

In spite of these difficulties quite a number of names may be said to have been satisfactorily identified. And any day may bring a new discovery which will furnish more evidence—a pot perhaps with its name duly inscribed or a specific description by an author contemporary with the vases. In the meantime the intricacy of the subject has its fascination.

Thus Athenian vases—apart from their decorations—have a many-sided interest. As well-proportioned, effective utensils they make a valuable contribution in the field of art. They can teach us, in many original specimens, the Greek conceptions of form during three centuries. And they make a special appeal to our imagination because they played an active part in the life of the Greeks. Though they now rest quietly on the shelves of museum cases, they once led a busy existence. They were taken to and from the fountains, filled and refilled at the banquets, carried about by athletes, used by women during their toilet, and brought as gifts to brides; they performed a rôle in religious ceremonies, were taken by mourners to graves, and sent in ships to distant lands. It is true that the vases in a large museum are selected examples, high above the average. The ordinary pots of the poorer households were not so carefully made and finished, as we may learn by examining the material dug up during any excavation. It was only the richer households in Athens and in Etruria, Sicily, and the other localities which imported Athenian ware that could afford the more precious specimens. Fine pots like other good things were for the élite. But the cheaper ware was after all of the same type, it had the same forms and decorations, and it was made of the same fine red clay; it was only that the execution was more hasty. And so if we want to reconstruct the daily life in the city of Athens from the time of Solon to that of Plato we must imagine such pots being used in every household—the masterpieces by the wealthy, the less precious by the poor—adding with their gay red and black designs a colorful note to the activities of the home and of out-of-doors.

KEY TO TERMS USED IN DESCRIBING SHAPES

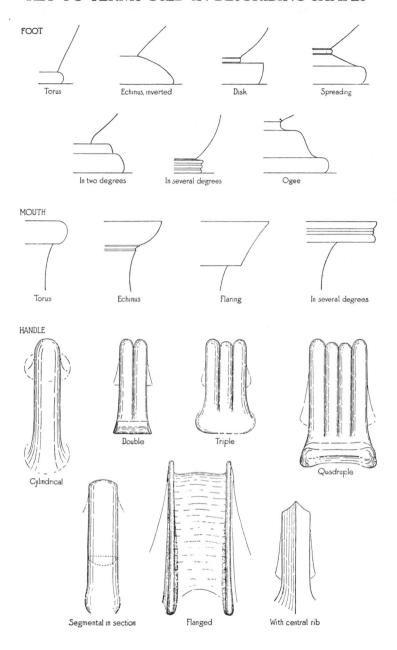

FOOT

Torus   Echinus, inverted   Disk   Spreading

In two degrees   In several degrees   Ogee

MOUTH

Torus   Echinus   Flaring   In several degrees

HANDLE

Cylindrical   Double   Triple   Quadruple

Segmental in section   Flanged   With central rib

RIDGE: Produced sometimes by applying a roll of clay, sometimes by tooling during the "turning" process.

LIST OF ABBREVIATIONS

The following abbreviations are used in the text and in the pages of illustrations:

A. J. A.—*American Journal of Archaeology.*
Ath. Mitt.—*Mitteilungen des deutschen archäologischen Instituts, Athenische Abteilung.*
B. C. H.—*Bulletin de correspondance hellénique.*
B. S. A.— *The Annual of the British School at Athens.*
C. I. G.—*Corpus inscriptionum Graecarum.*
C. V.—*Corpus vasorum antiquorum.*
I. G.—*Inscriptiones Graecae.*
J. H. S.—*The Journal of Hellenic Studies.*
Röm. Mitt.—*Mitteilungen des deutschen archäologischen Instituts, Römische Abteilung.*

———

Athens—National Museum, Athens.
Berlin—Staatliche Museen, Berlin.
Boston—Museum of Fine Arts, Boston.
Brussels—Musées Royaux d'Art et d'Histoire, Parc du Cinquantenaire, Brussels.
Munich—Museum antiker Kleinkunst.
Oxford—Ashmolean Museum, Oxford.
Würzburg—Martin v. Wagner Museum, Würzburg

SELECTED BIBLIOGRAPHY[1]

GENERAL

LIDDELL, H. G., and SCOTT, R. *A Greek-English Lexicon*, *passim*. New York: 8th edition, 1897; Oxford: 9th edition from 1925.

STEPHANUS, H. *Thesaurus Graecae linguae*, revised by K. Hase and W. and L. Dindorf. Paris, 1831–1865.

———

BEAZLEY, J. D. *Attische Vasenmaler des rotfigurigen Stils*, pp. 1–4. Tübingen, 1925.

GERHARD, E. In *Annali dell' Instituto di corrispondenza archeologica*, 1831,vol. III, pp. 221 ff.; 1836, vol. VIII, pp. 147 ff.

————— *Berlin's antike Bildwerke*, vol. I, pp. 342 ff. Berlin, 1836.

JAHN, O. *Beschreibung der Vasensammlung König Ludwigs in der Pinakothek zu München*, pp. LXXXVI–C. Munich, 1854.

LAU, T., BRUNN, H., and KRELL, P. F. *Die griechischen Vasen, ihr Formen- und Decorationssystem*. Leipzig, 1877.

LETRONNE, J. A. *Observations philologiques et archéologiques sur les noms des vases grecs à l'occasion de l'ouvrage de M. Th. Panofka intitulé Recherches, etc.* Paris, 1833. (Reprinted from *Journal des savants*, May, July, October, November, December, 1833.)

—————[Review of E. Gerhard]. In *Journal des savants*, November, 1837, pp. 683–686, December, 1837, pp. 740–753; January, 1838, pp. 5–10.

PANOFKA, T. *Recherches sur les véritables noms des vases grecs et sur leurs différens usages d'après les témoignages des auteurs et des monumens anciens*. Paris, 1829.

PAYNE, H. *Necrocorinthia, a Study of Corinthian Art in the Archaic Period*, *passim*. Oxford, 1931.

PFUHL, E. *Malerei und Zeichnung der Griechen*, vol. I, pp. 46 f., 294–307, 403–409. Munich, 1923.

ROLFE, J. C. In *Harvard Studies in Classical Philology*, 1891, vol. II, pp. 89 ff.

SMITH, W. *A Dictionary of Greek and Roman Antiquity*, vols. I, II, *passim*. 3d edition, revised by W. Wayte and G. E. Marindin. London, 1890–1891.

USSING, J. L. *De nominibus vasorum Graecorum disputatio*. Copenhagen, 1844.

WALTERS, H. B. *History of Ancient Pottery, Greek, Etruscan, and Roman*, vol. I, pp. 148–201. New York, 1905.

ANCIENT SOURCES

(Including Byzantine dictionaries based on the works of ancient lexicographers)

Athenaios Δειπνοσοφισταί, *passim*, especially Book XI (authors who are quoted by Athenaios are usually referred to in that context).

Ἐτυμολογικὸν μέγα (*Etymologicum magnum*).

Harpokration Λέξεις τῶν δέκα ῥητόρων.

---

[1] Not all the references cited in the text have been included in this reading list.

Hesychios Συναγωγὴ πασῶν λέξεων κατὰ στοιχεῖον.

Macrobius *Saturnalia* V. 21.

Moiris 'Αττικιστής.

Photios Λέξεων συναγωγή.

Pollux 'Ονομαστικόν, especially VI. 95 ff. and X. 62 ff.

Scholia on Aristophanes.

Suidas *Lexicon*.

Inscriptiones Graecae, Berlin: 1st edition from 1873; 2d edition from 1929.

Inscriptions de Délos (Académie des inscriptions et belles-lettres: Fonds d'épigraphie grecque— Fondation du duc de Loubac), edited by Félix Durrbach. Paris, from 1926. For Delian inscriptions cf. also *Bulletin de correspondance hellénique, passim*.

PROPORTIONS

CASKEY, L. D. *Geometry of Greek Vases*. Boston, 1922.

HAMBIDGE, J. *Dynamic Symmetry: the Greek Vase*. New Haven and New York, 1920.

RICHTER, I. A. *Rhythmic Form in Art*, pp. 47–61. London, 1932.

HANDLES

JACOBSTHAL, P. *Ornamente griechischer Vasen*, pp. 13–19. Berlin, 1927.

ALABASTRON

MAU, A. In A. Pauly and G. Wissowa, *Real-Encyclopädie der classischen Altertumswissenschaft*, *s. v.* alabastron. Stuttgart, 1894.

SAGLIO, E. In C. Daremberg and E. Saglio, *Dictionnaire des antiquités grecques et romaines*, vol. I, part 1, *s. v.* alabaster ou alabastrum. Paris, 1877.

SETHE, K. In *Sitzungsberichte der preussischen Akademie der Wissenschaften, Philosophisch-historische Klasse*, 1933, pp. 887–889.

AMPHORA (Including Pelike)

BEAZLEY, J. D. In *The Annual of the British School at Athens*, 1911–1912, vol. XVIII, pp. 217–219 (neck-amphora); 1912–1913, vol. XIX, pp. 239 f. (Panathenaic).

———— In *The Journal of Hellenic Studies*, 1914, vol. XXXIV, pp. 185 f.; 1922, vol. XLII, pp. 70 f. (amphora with neck and body forming continuous curve).

———— *Attic Red-figured Vases in American Museums*, pp. 37 f. (Nolan), p. 56 (pelike). Cambridge (Mass.), 1918.

———— *Greek Vases in Poland*, p. 7 note (Nolan). Oxford, 1928.

———— *Der Berliner Maler*, p. 11 (Nolan). Berlin, 1930.

BRAUCHITSCH, G. von. *Die Panathenäischen Preisamphoren*. Leipzig and Berlin, 1910.

BUSCHOR, E. In A. Furtwängler and K. Reichhold, *Griechische Vasenmalerei*, series III, p. 152 (late pelike). Munich, 1932.

GARDINER, E. N. In *The Journal of Hellenic Studies*, 1912, vol. XXXII, pp. 179–193 (Panathenaic).

LANGLOTZ, E. *Fruehgriechische Bildhauerschulen*, pp. 14 ff., pl. 13 (amphora with neck and body forming continuous curve). Nuremberg, 1927.

LUCE, S. B. In *American Journal of Archaeology*, 1916, vol. XX, pp. 439–459 (Nolan).

Morel, C. In C. Daremberg and E. Saglio, *Dictionnaire des antiquités grecques et romaines*, vol. I, part 1, *s. v.* amphora. Paris, 1877.

Robinson, D. M. *Corpus vasorum antiquorum: United States of America—The Robinson Collection, Baltimore, Md.*, fasc. 1, pp. 46 ff. (Panathenaic). Cambridge (Mass.), 1934.

Schmidt, E. *Archaistische Kunst in Griechenland und Rom*, pp. 70–91 (Panathenaic). Munich, 1922.

Wernicke, K. In A. Pauly and G. Wissowa, *Real-Encyclopädie der classischen Altertums-wissenschaft*, vol. I, *s. v.* amphora. Stuttgart, 1894.

ARYBALLOS

Beazley, J. D. In *The Annual of the British School at Athens*, 1927–1928, vol. XXIX, pp. 187 ff.

Haspels, C. H. E. In *The Annual of the British School at Athens*, 1927–1928, vol. XXIX, pp. 216 ff.

Robert, C. In A. Pauly and G. Wissowa, *Real-Encyclopädie der classischen Altertumswissen-schaft*, vol. II, *s. v.* aryballos. Stuttgart, 1896.

Saglio, E. In C. Daremberg and E. Saglio, *Dictionnaire des antiquités grecques et romaines*, vol. I, part 1, *s. v.* aryballos. Paris, 1877.

ASKOS

Beazley, J. D. In *American Journal of Archaeology*, 1921, vol. XXV, pp. 325 ff.

For varieties of the form not treated in the present work see:

Frankenstein, L. In A. Pauly and G. Wissowa, *Real-Encyclopädie der classischen Alter-tumswissenschaft*, suppl. vol. III, *s. v.* askos. Stuttgart, 1918.

Mayer, M. In *Jahrbuch des deutschen archäologischen Instituts*, 1907, vol. XXII, pp. 207 ff.

Pottier, E. In C. Daremberg and E. Saglio, *Dictionnaire des antiquités grecques et romaines*, vol. II, part 2, *s. v.* guttus. Paris, 1896.

Snijder, G. A. S. In *Mnemosyne*, 1933–1934, 3d series, vol. I, pp. 34 ff.

Zahn, R. In A. Pauly and G. Wissowa, *op. cit.*, vol. VII, *s. v.* guttus. Stuttgart, 1912.

VASES IN THE FORM OF HUMAN HEADS

Beazley, J. D. In *The Journal of Hellenic Studies*, 1929, vol. XLIX, pp. 38 ff.

Buschor, E. In *Münchner Jahrbuch der bildenden Kunst*, vol. XI, part 1–2 [1919], pp. 9 ff.

HYDRIA

Beazley, J. D. *Attic Red-figured Vases in American Museums*, p. 61. Cambridge (Mass.), 1918.

Buschor, E. In A. Furtwängler and K. Reichhold, *Griechische Vasenmalerei*, series III, p. 152. Munich, 1932.

Couve, L. In C. Daremberg and E. Saglio, *Dictionnaire des antiquités grecques et romaines*, vol. III, part 1, *s. v.* kalpis. Paris, 1899.

Fölzer, E. *Die Hydria, ein Beitrag zur griechischen Vasenkunde (Beiträge zur Kunstgeschichte, n. s. no. XXXIII)*. Leipzig, 1906.

FRANKENSTEIN, L. In A. Pauly and G. Wissowa, *Real-Encyclopädie der classischen Altertums-wissenschaft*, vol. IX, cols. 2516 ff., *s. v.* hydria. Stuttgart, 1916.

POTTIER, E. In Daremberg and Saglio, *op. cit., s. v.* hydria.

KALATHOS

BEAZLEY, J. D. In *The Journal of Hellenic Studies*, 1931, vol. LI, p. 56, no. 16.

FURTWÄNGLER, A. In A. Furtwängler and K. Reichhold, *Griechische Vasenmalerei*, series II, pl. 64. Munich, 1909.

HUG, A. In A. Pauly and G. Wissowa, *Real-Encyclopädie der classischen Altertumswissen-schaft*, vol. X, *s. v.* kalathos. Stuttgart, 1919.

SAGLIO, E. In C. Daremberg and E. Saglio, *Dictionnaire des antiquités grecques et romaines*, vol. I, part 2, *s. v.* calathus. Paris [n. d.].

KANTHAROS

BEAZLEY, J. D. *Greek Vases in Poland*, p. 28. Oxford, 1928.

CASKEY, L. D. (with the coöperation of J. D. Beazley). *Attic Vase Paintings in the Museum of Fine Arts, Boston*, pp. 14–18. London and Boston, 1931.

FRANKENSTEIN, L. In A. Pauly and G. Wissowa, *Real-Encyclopädie der classischen Altertums-wissenschaft*, suppl. vol. IV, *s. v.* kantharos. Stuttgart, 1924.

SAGLIO, E. In C. Daremberg and E. Saglio, *Dictionnaire des antiquités grecques et romaines*, vol. I, part 2, *s. v.* cantharus. Paris [n. d.].

KRATER

ANGER, I. In A. Pauly and G. Wissowa, *Real-Encyclopädie der classischen Altertumswissen-schaft*, vol. XV, *s. v.* Mischkrug. Stuttgart, 1932.

BEAZLEY, J. D. In *The Journal of Hellenic Studies*, 1911, vol. XXXI, p. 283 (bell krater).

————— *Attic Red-figured Vases in American Museums*, pp. 41 f. (calyx krater), p. 114 (bell krater). Cambridge (Mass.), 1918.

————— *Greek Vases in Poland*, p. 54, note 4 (bell krater with lugs). Oxford, 1928.

BUSCHOR, E. In A. Furtwängler and K. Reichhold, *Griechische Vasenmalerei*, series III, pp. 152 ff. (calyx krater and bell krater). Munich, 1932.

JACOBSTHAL, P. In *Metropolitan Museum Studies*, 1934, vol. V, part 1, pp. 117 ff. (calyx krater).

POTTIER, E. In C. Daremberg and E. Saglio, *Dictionnaire des antiquités grecques et romaines*, vol. I, part 2, *s. v.* crater. Paris [n. d.].

ZAHN, R. In Furtwängler and Reichhold, *op. cit.*, series III, pp. 204 f. (calyx krater).

KYATHOS

LEONARD, F. In A. Pauly and G. Wissowa, *Real-Encyclopädie der classischen Altertums-wissenschaft*, vol. XI, *s. v.* kyathos. Stuttgart, 1922.

POTTIER, E. In C. Daremberg and E. Saglio, *Dictionnaire des antiquités grecques et romaines*, vol. I, part 2, *s. v.* cyathus. Paris [n. d.].

KYLIX

BEAZLEY, J. D. In *The Journal of Hellenic Studies*, 1931, vol. LI, pp. 275 ff. ("Siana" cups); 1932, vol. LII, pp. 167 ff.

———— In *Metropolitan Museum Studies*, 1934, vol. V, part 1, pp. 93, 102 ff. ("Siana" cups).

BEAZLEY, J. D., and PAYNE, H. In *The Journal of Hellenic Studies*, 1929, vol. XLIX, p. 260 and *passim* ("Siana" cups, etc.).

NACHOD, H. In A. Pauly and G. Wissowa, *Real-Encyclopädie der classischen Altertums-wissenschaft*, suppl. vol. V, *s. v.* kylix. Stuttgart, 1931.

SAGLIO, E. In C. Daremberg and E. Saglio, *Dictionnaire des antiquités grecques et romaines*, vol. I, part 2, *s. v.* calix. Paris [n. d.].

LEBES

ANGER, I. In A. Pauly and G. Wissowa, *Real-Encyclopädie der classischen Altertumswissen-schaft*, vol. XV, cols. 2033 f., *s. v.* Mischkrug. Stuttgart, 1932.

POTTIER, E. In C. Daremberg and E. Saglio, *Dictionnaire des antiquités grecques et romaines*, vol. I, part 2, *s. v.* crater. Paris [n. d.].

RIDDER, A. DE. In C. Daremberg and E. Saglio, *op. cit.*, vol. III, part 2, *s. v.* lébès. Paris, 1904.

ROBERT, C. In A. Pauly and G. Wissowa, *op. cit.*, vol. V, *s. v.* dinos. Stuttgart, 1905.

LEBES GAMIKOS

BRUECKNER, A. In *Mitteilungen des deutschen archäologischen Instituts, Athenische Abteilung*, 1907, vol. XXXII, pp. 91 ff.

HARTWIG, P. In *Ephemeris Archaiologike*, 1897, cols. 136 ff.; 1899, col. 55.

LEKANIS

COUVE, L. In C. Daremberg and E. Saglio, *Dictionnaire des antiquités grecques et romaines*, vol. III, part 2, *s. v.* lékané. Paris, 1904.

DEUBNER, L. In *Jahrbuch des deutschen archäologischen Instituts*, 1900, vol. XV, p. 152.

NACHOD, H. In A. Pauly and G. Wissowa, *Real-Encyclopädie der classischen Altertums-wissenschaft*, vol. XIII, cols. 2559 f., *s. v.* lekane. Stuttgart, 1927.

STEPHANI, L. In *Compte-rendu de la Commission impériale archéologique pour l'année 1860*, pp. 5 ff.

URE, A. D. In *Metropolitan Museum Studies*, 1932, vol. IV, part 1, p. 18.

LEKYTHOS

ELFERINK, L. J. *Lekythos (Allard Pierson Stichting, Universiteit van Amsterdam: Archaeolo-gisch-historische Bijdragen, no. II)*. Amsterdam, 1934.

FAIRBANKS, A. *Athenian Lekythoi with Outline Drawing in Glaze Varnish on a White Ground (University of Michigan Studies: Humanistic Series, vol. VI)*, pp. 9–12. New York, 1907.

LANGLOTZ, E. In *Philologische Wochenschrift*, 1923, vol. XLIII, col. 1025.

———— *Griechische Vasen (Martin von Wagner-Museum der Universität Würzburg)*, p. 69. Munich, 1932.

NACHOD, H. In A. Pauly and G. Wissowa, *Real-Encyclopädie der classischen Altertums-wissenschaft*, suppl. vol. V, *s. v.* lekythos. Stuttgart, 1931.

POTTIER, E. In C. Daremberg and E. Saglio, *Dictionnaire des antiquités grecques et romaines*, vol. III, part 2, *s. v.* lecythus. Paris, 1904.

RIEZLER, W. *Weissgrundige attische Lekythen*. Munich, 1914.

LOUTROPHOROS

BEAZLEY, J. D. *Greek Vases in Poland*, p. 42, note 6 (loutrophoros-hydria). Oxford, 1928.

———— In *The Museum Journal* (University of Pennsylvania) [1932–1933], vol. XXIII, pp. 5, 14 ff. ("battle loutrophoros").

BRUECKNER, A. and PERNICE, E. In *Mitteilungen des deutschen archäologischen Instituts, Athenische Abteilung*, 1893, vol. XVIII, pp. 144 ff.

COLLIGNON, M. In C. Daremberg and E. Saglio, *Dictionnaire des antiquités grecques et romaines*, vol. III, part 2, *s. v.* loutrophoros. Paris, 1904.

HERZOG, A. In *Archäologische Zeitung*, 1882, vol. XL, cols. 131 ff.

MILCHHOEFER, A. In *Mitteilungen des deutschen archäologischen Instituts, Athenische Abteilung*, 1880, vol. V, pp. 174 ff.

NACHOD, H. In A. Pauly and G. Wissowa, *Real-Encyclopädie der classischen Altertumswissenschaft*, vol. XIII, *s. v.* lutrophoros. Stuttgart, 1927.

WOLTERS, P. In *Mitteilungen des deutschen archäologischen Instituts, Athenische Abteilung*, 1891, vol. XVI, pp. 371 ff.

———— In *Jahrbuch des deutschen archäologischen Instituts*, 1899, vol. XIV, pp. 133 f.

MASTOS

NACHOD, H. In A. Pauly and G. Wissowa, *Real-Encyclopädie der classischen Altertumswissenschaft*, vol. XIV, *s. v.* mastos. Stuttgart, 1930.

POTTIER, E. In C. Daremberg and E. Saglio, *Dictionnaire des antiquités grecques et romaines*, vol. III, part 2, *s. v.* mastos. Paris, 1904.

OINOCHOE

CASKEY, L. D. (with the coöperation of J. D. Beazley). *Attic Vase Paintings in the Museum of Fine Arts, Boston*, p. 40. London and Boston, 1931.

DEUBNER, L. *Attische Feste*, pp. 96 ff. Berlin, 1932.

KARO, G. In C. Daremberg and E. Saglio, *Dictionnaire des antiquités grecques et romaines*, vol. IV, part 1, *s. v.* oinochoé. Paris [n. d.].

PFUHL, E. *Malerei und Zeichnung der Griechen*, vol. II, p. 518 (bibliography on toy oinochoai). Munich, 1923.

PELIKE. See under Amphora

PHIALE

POTTIER, E. In C. Daremberg and E. Saglio, *Dictionnaire des antiquités grecques et romaines*, vol. IV, part 1, *s. v.* phiala. Paris [n. d.].

PLEMOCHOE

BURROWS, R. M., and URE, P. N. In *The Journal of Hellenic Studies*, 1911, vol. XXXI, pp. 76, 86 ff., 96.

CASKEY, L. D. (with the coöperation of J. D. Beazley). *Attic Vase Paintings in the Museum of Fine Arts, Boston*, pp. 49 f. London and Boston, 1931.

LEONARD, F. In A. Pauly and G. Wissowa, *Real-Encyclopädie der classischen Altertumswissenschaft*, vol. XI, *s. v.* kothon, cols. 1519 f. Stuttgart, 1922.

MICHEL, C. In C. Daremberg and E. Saglio, *Dictionnaire des antiquités grecques et romaines*, vol. IV, part 1, *s. v.* plémochoé. Paris [n. d.].

PERNICE, E. In *Jahrbuch des deutschen archäologischen Instituts*, 1899, vol. XIV, pp. 67 ff.

PFUHL, E. In *Jahrbuch des deutschen archäologischen Instituts*, 1912, vol. XXVII, pp. 52 ff.

ROBINSON, E. In *Trustees of the Museum of Fine Arts* [Boston] *Twenty-fourth Annual Report, for the Year . . . 1899*, pp. 73 ff.

PSYKTER

BEAZLEY, J. D. *Attic Red-figured Vases in American Museums*, p. 28. Cambridge (Mass.), 1918.

KARO, G. In *The Journal of Hellenic Studies*, 1899, vol. XIX, p. 141.

————— In C. Daremberg and E. Saglio, *Dictionnaire des antiquités grecques et romaines*, vol. IV, part 1, *s. v.* psykter. Paris [n. d.].

PYXIS

CASKEY, L. D. (with the coöperation of J. D. Beazley). *Attic Vase Paintings in the Museum of Fine Arts, Boston*, pp. 35 f. London and Boston, 1931.

CURTIUS, L. In 88. *Winckelmannsprogramm der archäologischen Gesellschaft zu Berlin*, pp. 1 ff. Berlin and Leipzig, 1929.

POTTIER, E. In C. Daremberg and E. Saglio, *Dictionnaire des antiquités grecques et romaines*, vol. IV, part 1, *s. v.* pyxis. Paris [n. d.].

RHYTON

BUSCHOR, E. In *Münchner Jahrbuch der bildenden Kunst*, vol. XI, part 1–2 [1919], pp. 15 ff.

FRANKENSTEIN, L. In A. Pauly and G. Wissowa, *Real-Encyclopädie der classischen Altertumswissenschaft*, vol. XI, *s. v.* keras. Stuttgart, 1922.

POTTIER, E. In C. Daremberg and E. Saglio, *Dictionnaire des antiquités grecques et romaines*, vol. IV, part 2, *s. v.* rhyton. Paris [n. d.].

SKYPHOS

BUSCHOR, E. In A. Furtwängler and K. Reichhold, *Griechische Vasenmalerei*, series III, pp. 124 f. Munich, 1932.

LEONARD, F. In A. Pauly and G. Wissowa, *Real-Encyclopädie der classischen Altertumswissenschaft*, vol. XI, *s. v.* kotyle. Stuttgart, 1922.

NACHOD, H. In Pauly and Wissowa, *op. cit.*, 2d series, vol. III, *s. v.* skyphos. Stuttgart, 1929.

POTTIER, E. In C. Daremberg and E. Saglio, *Dictionnaire des antiquités grecques et romaines*, vol. I, part 2, *s. v.* cotyla; vol. IV, part 2, *s. v.* scyphus. Paris [n. d.].

STAMNOS

BEAZLEY, J. D. *Attic Red-figured Vases in American Museums*, p. 40. Cambridge (Mass.), 1918.

LANGLOTZ, E. *Fruehgriechische Bildhauerschulen*, pp. 18 ff., pl. 14. Nuremberg, 1927.

NACHOD, H. In A. Pauly and G. Wissowa, *Real-Encyclopädie der classischen Altertumswissenschaft*, series II, vol. III, *s. v.* stamnos. Stuttgart, 1929.

POTTIER, E. In C. Daremberg and E. Saglio, *Dictionnaire des antiquités grecques et romaines*, vol. IV, part 2, *s. v.* stamnos. Paris [n. d.].

VASES IN THE METROPOLITAN MUSEUM OF ART

FIGURED IN

"SHAPES AND NAMES OF ATHENIAN VASES"

SHAPES AND NAMES
OF
ATHENIAN VASES

SHAPES AND NAMES OF ATHENIAN VASES

AMPHORA (Greek ἀμφορεύς, old form ἀμφιφορεύς; from ἀμφί, on both sides, and φέρω, carry[1]). Jar with two handles reaching from mouth or neck to body. Used for holding provisions. Figs. 1–35.

According to Athenaios (XI.501 a) the amphora "could be carried on either side by the handles." Aischylos (Frag. 108) refers to one as "narrow-mouthed," στενόστομον. We learn that it was used for both liquid and solid provisions: "The amphorae are full of red and fragrant wine" (Aristophanes *Ploutos* 807); "drinking a whole amphora of milk" (Euripides *Cyclops* 327); "they found pickled slices of dolphins in amphorae" (Xenophon *Anabasis* V.4.28). It was also used as a measure: "The silver krater (*sc.* one dedicated by Kroisos at Delphi) holding 600 amphorae" (Herodotos I.51).

Amphorae filled with oil were given as prizes at the Panathenaic festival celebrated once every four years in Athens: "At the Panathenaic games he won five garlands, sixty amphorae full of oil" (Pseudo-Simonides Frag. 147, Diehl); "in earth baked by fire came the fruit of the olive in richly painted walls of vases" (Pindar *Nemean* X.35 f., speaking of athletic victories won in Athens). We learn from an inscription (*I.G.*,II, 965 = Dittenberger, *Sylloge*[3], 1055) that as many as 140 amphorae full of oil might be given as one prize at these games. As extant examples of this class of amphora can be identified from the inscription on them, "one of the prizes from Athens" (cf. p. 4), we have conclusive evidence that the shape here discussed was called amphora.[2]

In Greek vase paintings vases of this shape frequently appear as wine or oil jars (see illustrations on pp. 5, 9, 24), but occasionally for carrying water.

There are two chief types of amphora: with neck and body forming a continuous curve, and with neck set off from body.

TYPE I. Neck and body forming continuous curve.

---

[1] Derivations are given in this book only when they are not open to question (except in the case of the alabastron, cf. p. 17).

[2] The Scholiast on the passage in Pindar, however, refers to the prize vases as hydriai, quoting Kallimachos, who uses the word kalpis. The confusion is perhaps due to the fact that hydriai were evidently also given as prizes at the Panathenaic games; in the inscription quoted above a hydria is listed as a prize for the torch race (for representations of the torch-race hydria cf. Beazley, *Greek Vases in Poland*, pp. 20, 79). But a more plausible explanation is that given by Stephani (*Compte-rendu de la Commission impériale archéologique*, 1876, pp. 32 f.) that Kallimachos refers to hydriai in which wrestlers' lots were placed.

3

(a) Lip flaring, and straight to slightly concave; handles cylindrical in section; foot shaped like an inverted echinus (cf. figs. 1–5). The form occurs from the late seventh century to the third quarter of the fifth.

(b) Lip flaring and slightly concave; flat handles with flanges; foot in two parts, the lower of convex outline (cf. figs. 6–8). The type occurs from the middle of the sixth century to about 450.

(c) Similar to I a, but with convex, slightly spreading mouth and either torus or echinus foot (cf. figs. 9–11). The form occurs, especially in the second quarter of the sixth century, in the black-figured "affected" amphorae, and in red-figure from about 520 to 470.

Type II. Neck set off from body ("neck-amphora").

(a) Lip echinus-shaped, torus foot (cf. figs. 12–19). In the earlier examples the forms of mouth and foot vary; but the shape when once evolved was standardized and enjoyed a great popularity during the late period of black-figure.

A special form of this type is the Nolan amphora (so called from Nola, in South Italy, where many such examples have been found). The form is popular in red-figure during the first half of the fifth century and lasts into the second half. Generally speaking, the handles of the earlier examples are triple, and those of the later ones have a central rib.

(b) Elongated body; handles usually twisted; mouth generally in two degrees, the lower echinus-shaped; foot in two degrees, the lower of convex profile; ridge at base of body (cf. figs. 20–23). The type appears about 500 and lasts into the fourth century.

(c) Panathenaic form, used as a prize at the Panathenaic games. Broad body tapering sharply downward, handles cylindrical in section (cf. figs. 24–27). The shape is not confined to the prize vases, but only on the latter does the inscription "one of the prizes from Athens" occur. The extant examples range in date from about 560 to the third century.[3]

(d) Body pointed at bottom so that it could be set in a stand; handles mostly cylindrical in section; ridge at base of neck (cf. figs. 28–31). The form is often represented on vases (see illustrations on pp. 5, 9, 24).

There are also several less common variations of type II (cf. figs. 32–35).

PELIKE (Greek πελίκη). A variety of amphora with the widest portion toward the base and a broad neck forming a continuous curve with the body. Figs. 36–39.

---

[3] The gap that used to be assumed during the fifth century has been bridged. See Gardiner, *J. H. S.*, 1912, vol. XXXII, pp. 184–188; Schmidt, *Archaistische Kunst*, pp. 70 ff.; Pfuhl, *Malerei und Zeichnung der Griechen*, vol. I, pp. 332 f.; Robinson, *C. V.: U. S. A.—Robinson Coll.*, pp. 46 ff. (on this cf. Beazley, review, *J. H. S.*, 1934, vol. LIV, pp. 89 f.).

The application of the name to vases of this shape has no justification. It was used by early archaeologists and is now kept for convenience.

The Greek πελίκη is described variously by ancient authors: as a kylix by Kallistratos (in Athenaios XI.495 a); as a chous by Krates of Mallos[4]—who adds that earlier it had the form of the Panathenaic vases but later took the shape of the oinochoe used in the festival (of the Choes); as a lekane, in Boeotian, by Photios (s.v. πελίχαν; cf. Pollux X.78).

The form first appears at the end of the sixth century and lasts through the fourth.

Youth with amphora and kylix. From a column krater in the Metropolitan Museum. About 480

LOUTROPHOROS (Greek λουτροφόρος, from λουτρόν, bath, and φέρω, bring). Tall vase with high, funnel-shaped neck, slender body, and flaring mouth. Water was brought in it from the fountain Kallirrhoe for the nuptial bath, and it was placed on tombs of unmarried persons. Figs. 40-42.

Harpokration defines a loutrophoros as follows (s.v. λουτροφόρος καὶ λουτροφορεῖν): "It was the custom at marriage to send for a bath on the wedding day; for this purpose they sent the boy who was the nearest relative and these boys brought the bath. And it was also the custom to put a loutrophoros on the tomb of those who died unwed."[5] Hesychios (s.v. λουτρο-

[4] Or Krates of Athens? Cf. Jacoby in Pauly-Wissowa, Real-Encyclopädie, s.v. Krates (12).

[5] His further statement that the "loutrophoros" placed on the tomb was a statue of a boy (for whom Pollux VIII.66 substitutes a girl) carrying a hydria is apparently an error; cf. Herzog, Archäologische Zeitung, 1882, vol. XL, col. 138.

φόρα ἄγγη) describes "loutrophoros vases" as hydriai sent to those who died unmarried and also to weddings. Pseudo-Demosthenes (XLIV. 18) has a significant passage: "Archiades died unmarried. And the proof? A loutrophoros stands on his tomb."

Vases of this shape are regularly decorated with funerary or marriage scenes, and representations of them appear in scenes of weddings and funerals

Mourning women, one carrying a loutrophoros.
Detail of fig. 40. About 500

(see illustrations on pp. 6, 10, 23). A few loutrophoroi have battle scenes, presumably to commemorate dead soldiers.

On this evidence the name loutrophoros has been convincingly applied to the shape.

Two forms occur, one a kind of amphora, in which the two tall handles often have extra supports (cf. figs. 40, 42); the other a kind of hydria with three handles (cf. fig. 41).

KRATER (Greek κρατήρ, from κεράννυμι, mix). Vessel with deep, broad body and wide mouth. Used for mixing wine and water. Figs. 43–63.

In Odysseus' house attendants are "mixing wine and water in kraters" for the suitors (*Odyssey* I.110). "They are mixing kraters (of wine)," announces the herald in Aristophanes' *Ekklesiazousai* (841), as he summons the

6

citizens to a public banquet. Suidas (*s.v.* κρατήρ) also associates the krater with dining.

We know that the Greeks rarely drank their wine neat—a favorite proportion was one part of wine to three parts of water (cf. Hesychios, *s.v.* ἄρ᾽ οἴσει τρία)—and there are numerous representations on vases which show vessels of the shape here discussed serving as wine bowls (see illustrations on pp. 7, 13).

On this evidence the name krater has been convincingly applied to the shape.

Photograph by Marie Beazley

Boy dipping his jug into a column krater to ladle wine into cups. From a cup by Epiktetos in the Ashmolean Museum, Oxford, no. 520. End of sixth century

The usual Attic name for the stand of a krater is ὑπόστατον (cf. e. g. I. G., II–III², 1421, 19; Pollux X.79).

There are several forms of krater—the column krater, the volute krater, the calyx krater, the bell krater. Their ancient names have not been identified.

COLUMN KRATER. So called from the columnar shape of the handles (cf. figs. 43–48). Each handle consists of a pair of cylindrical stems terminating in a horizontal member joined to the rim. The outer part of the lip, of slightly concave outline, hangs over the neck. The shape, used from the first half of the sixth century, is a favorite till the third quarter of the fifth, and then loses its popularity.

VOLUTE KRATER. So called from the shape of the handles (cf. figs. 49–54). Each handle is in the form of a spiral with flanged sides rising from loops on the shoulder to above the rim. The mouth is only slightly set off from the wide neck. The shape is in use from the first half of the sixth century through the fifth and fourth centuries.

CALYX KRATER. With body in the shape of the calyx of a flower (cf. figs. 55–

7

59). Body in two parts, the lower convex, the upper slightly concave; handles, which are set at the top of the lower part, curve upward; no neck; foot in two degrees; ridge at base of body. The shape appears at the end of the sixth century in red-figured vases and lasts throughout the fourth.

BELL KRATER. In the form of an inverted bell, with loop handles placed high on the body and curving slightly upward (cf. figs. 60–63). The extant examples range in date from the early fifth century through the fourth.

Women ladling wine from a stamnos into cups. From a stamnos in the Metropolitan Museum. About 450–440

STAMNOS (Greek στάμνος, σταμνίον, etc.). High-shouldered, short-necked jar with two handles set horizontally. Used as a wine jar. Figs. 64–68.

The evidence for applying the name stamnos to this form is insufficient, but the name has been retained for convenience.

Aristophanes speaks of "a Thasian stamnion of wine" (*Lysistrata* 196) and of "Dionysos, son of Stamnios" (*Frogs* 22). Pseudo-Demosthenes (XXXV.32) refers to a shipment of wine from the north as "eighty stamnoi of sour wine." Moiris (*s.v.* ἀμφορέα) states that amphoreus was the Attic name for the two-handled stamnos, whereas the common Greek name was stamnos. It was also used for oil (Delian temple inventory, *B.C.H.*, 1890, vol. XIV, p. 413; *I.G.*, XI, 161, col. B, 123). Inscriptions mentioning sums of money kept in stamnoi have been found at Delos (Homolle, *B.C.H.*, 1882, vol. VI, pp. 6 ff., 60 ff.; Durrbach, *Inscriptions de Délos*, 442, col. A, 3 ff.; 399, col. A, 3 ff.). The stamnoi "with one handle" listed in a Delian inscription (*B.C.H.*, 1890, vol. XIV, p. 413; *I.G.*, XI, 161, B, 122 f.) had perhaps lost a handle, since many broken objects are listed in these inventories (*B.C.H.*, 1882, vol. VI, p. 119).

It seems probable on this evidence that stamnos was another name for a regular large amphora and does not denote the shape here described. The latter, however, was also used for wine, as is shown by representations on vases (see illustration on p. 8). The shape is prevalent from the end of the sixth century to the end of the fifth.

Chariot race at the funeral games of Patroklos. On the ground are a lebes and a tripod with lebes, the prizes for the victors. From the François vase, fig. 49. About 570–560

LEBES (Greek λέβης). Deep bowl with round bottom, made to be set on a stand. Figs. 69–71.

The lebes is thus described by Aischylos: "The three-footed lebes (τρί-

In the center is a lebes on a stand, which is being filled with wine from amphorae; two oinochoai for dipping out the wine into the cups are at hand. From a stamnos by Smikros in the Musée Cinquantenaire, Brussels, no. 2190. About 510–500

πους λέβης) of the house received him, the lebes that kept its station above the fire" (in Athenaios II.37 f). In the *Iliad* (XXIII.259) Achilles carries from the ships "the prizes—lebetes and tripods" to be used at the funeral games of Patroklos (see illustration above). On a fragment from a vase found on the Akropolis (Graef, *Die antiken Vasen von der Akropolis*, pl. 27 a) is a tripod with bowl inscribed "lebes"; it is one of the prizes given at the funeral games of Pelias. Lebetes also served for mixing wine, like the kraters (Semos of Delos in Athenaios II.38 a). In a Delian inscription (*I.G.*, XI, 161, B, 125) is mentioned a round krater with a stand (κρατὴρ στρογ- γύλος ὑπόστατον ἔχων), evidently a lebes.

Many examples of bronze bowls—either made in one piece with the tri- pod (cf. e. g. *Olympia*, vol. IV, pls. XXVII ff.; *Fouilles de Delphes*, vol. V, pp. 60 ff.) or separate (cf. *J.H.S.*, 1926, vol. XLVI, pl. XIV)—have been preserved. Vessels of this shape appear in vase paintings both as prizes given at the games (see illustration on p. 9) and as containers of wine in banquet scenes (see illustration on p. 9). The shape of these bowls is the same as

Furtwängler and Reichhold, *Griechische Vasenmalerei*, pl. 57, 3

A bride being dressed. A little maid is fastening her shoes while another is bringing her jewelry in a box. At the door stand two marriage vases filled with twigs, and a loutrophoros near by also contains branches. On a little chest stands a pyxis, or toilet box. A mirror hangs on the wall. From a pyxis in the British Museum, no. E 774. About 430

that illustrated in figs. 69–71. Probably the bronze bowls were used for cooking, whereas the terracotta ones served only for mixing wine, like the krater.

On this evidence the name lebes can confidently be applied to the shape

The name dinos (Greek δῖνος[6]) is also frequently applied to this shape. But the only information we have regarding the Greek dinos indicates that it was a cup. In a comic fragment in Athenaios (XI.467 d) one character lists the large dinos with skyphoi, rhyta, etc., and the other character re- marks, "The old woman won't look at anything but drinking cups!" Hesy- chios defines the dinos as "a kind of drinking cup" and Pollux (VI.96) classi- fies it with drinking cups. In Aristophanes' *Wasps* 616 ff., the context sug- gests that it was a cup.

[6] This is the spelling in Attic inscriptions (*I. G.*, II–III², 1534, 280, 324; 1695, 10, 11, both of the third century B.C.). The pun in Archedikos (Frag. 1, Kock) which Eustathios quotes as evidence for the spelling δεῖνος refers to a vulgar itacistic pronunciation of the adjective δεινός.

LEBES GAMIKOS (Greek λέβης γαμικός). "Marriage bowl." High foot, double handles on the shoulder, the bowl in one piece with the foot. Figs. 72–75.

A temple inventory found at Eleusis mentions lebetes gamikoi, probably of bronze (*I.G.*, II–III², 1544, 63; Hartwig, quoting Zahn, *Ephemeris Archaiologike*, 1899, col. 55). Since the shape here illustrated is a "lebes" on a foot and vases of this shape appear in representations of marriage ceremonies (see illustrations on pp. 10, 23), the identification seems justified. Evidently λέβης νυμφικός, which occurs in an Attic inscription (*I.G.*, II–III², 1471, 44), is another name for the same shape.

Hoppin, *Euthymides and His Fellows*, pl. 36

Two girls fetching water from a fountain. The girl at the left is about to lift her jar to her head. The other is putting the little cushion for protection on her head, meanwhile holding her dress away from the water. From a hydria in the Torlonia Collection, Rome. About 500

HYDRIA (Greek ὑδρία, from ὕδωρ, water). Water jar with three handles. The vertical handle at the back was used for carrying the vessel or for pouring; the horizontal handles at the sides, for lifting. Figs. 76–86.

In a representation on the François vase of Achilles pursuing Troilos (Furtwängler and Reichhold, *Griechische Vasenmalerei*, pls. 11, 12) is a jar of this shape, with neck set off from body, inscribed ὑδρία.[7] Vases of this shape often appear in scenes of women carrying water from a fountain (see illustration above). It is therefore obvious that they were used as water jars. This, of course, does not preclude other uses. For instance, we learn from Xenophon (*Hellenika* I.vii.9) that hydriai were used as ballot boxes; from Isokrates (XVII.33) that they served as urns for depositing the names

[7] The artist evidently neglected to add the vertical handle; all three handles appear in another jar of this shape in the same scene. Similarly, in our illustration above of girls at the fountain the horizontal handles on one of the hydriai have been omitted; cf. Pfuhl, *Malerei und Zeichnung der Griechen*, III, figs. 296, 382.

of judges: "For who of you does not know that Pythodoros . . . last year opened the hydriai and took out the (names of the) judges placed in them by the Boule."They also made convenient cinerary urns; in a cemetery at Hadra, near Alexandria, many hydriai were found used as urns for the ashes of the dead. Apparently the word could be applied to any vessel containing water (cf. e.g. Hesychios: ἀσκός· ὑδρία).[8]

There are two distinct types of hydria, one with the neck set off from the body, the other with the neck forming a continuous curve with the body. The latter is often called kalpis (Greek κάλπις) by archaeologists; but there is no evidence for this distinction. Kalpis and hydria are used interchangeably by Aristophanes in *Lysistrata* 327 and 358, and by Plutarch in *Demetrios* 53; but no specific information is given regarding their forms. Kalpis is said to be a Thessalian word for hydria (Bekker's *Anecdota* 1095). It is used by Korinna (Frag. 4, l. 20, Diehl) of the golden urns in which the gods, at the singing match between Kithairon and Helikon, placed their votes. It occurs in the *Odyssey* and in Pindar and the Attic poets for water jar. In Antiphanes (fourth century b.c.) and Polybios the kalpis is used for perfume lavishly distributed, so it may here too be identical with the hydria. It is described as a cup by Philemon (in Athenaios XI.468 e, f; cf. Athenaios XI.475 c and Hesychios, *s.v.* κάλπος). Apparently the word is a poetic one, possibly Aeolic in origin, and usually, at least, means a water jar.

TYPE I, with neck set off from body (cf. figs. 76–79), is prevalent during the sixth century.

TYPE II, with neck, shoulder, and body forming a continuous curve ("kalpis") (cf. figs. 80–86), appears at the end of the sixth century and continues through the fourth.

PSYKTER (Greek ψυκτήρ, from ψύχω, cool). Vase for cooling wine. Figs. 87–89.

The psykter is defined by scholiasts and lexicographers as a cup (cf. Scholiast on Plato, *Symposion* 213; Hesychios). Passages in other writers, however, suggest a large vessel (cf. Kallixeinos in Athenaios V. 199 d, f; and references to inscriptions given by Karo in Daremberg and Saglio, *Dictionnaire*, *s.v.* psykter, p. 750, notes 13, 14); and since the name implies a cooler we may suppose that it was a largish container. The statement by Pollux (VI.99) that it held unmixed wine bears this out. The definition, cup, in the lexicographers may therefore be due to a misunderstanding of such passages as Plato's *Symposion* 213 e–214 a, where Alcibiades bids the boy bring him

[8] Cf. also Hesychios, *s. v.* ἀμφιφορεύς, where amphiphoreus is defined as both a coffin and a hydria.

a psykter—which held more than eight kotylai (over 3 pints)[9]—when the ordinary cups were insufficient (cf. also Menander, Frag. 510, Kock; Alexis, Frag. 9, Kock). Since descriptions of the shape of the psykter are contradictory ("having a foot,"[10] I.G., II–III², 1542, 22 f.; and "not having a foot,"[10] Pollux VI.99; "partly cylindrical and on a columnar base," Scholiast on Clement of Alexandria, p. 188; "with astragaliskoi," Pollux VI.99), we may infer that it was named for its function, not for its shape.

Cooling wine was a common practice with the Greeks. For instance Strattis (Frag. 57, Kock) says, "No one would be willing to drink his wine warm but on the contrary he wants it cooled in the well and mixed with snow." The form illustrated in figs. 87, 88, a high-stemmed bowl with narrow mouth and broad body drawn in toward the base, would be adapted for cooling wine. The cooling liquid would surround the vase, which was placed inside a krater full of cold water (see illustration at right), a use which explains the uncommon form. A psykter actually placed in a krater was found in an Etruscan tomb and is now in Florence (cf. Karo in Daremberg and Saglio, Dictionnaire, s.v. psykter, p. 750). It is therefore quite possible that this shape was one of the forms of the Greek psykter. Another terracotta form—an amphora with double walls in which the cooling liquid could be introduced into the outer compartment (cf. fig. 89) —evidently served the same purpose. Not

Ath. Mitt., 1889, pl. XIII. XIV

Boy ladling wine from a psykter placed in a krater. From an oinochoe in the National Museum, Athens, no. 1045 (CC. 691). Late sixth century

many examples of either type have been preserved. The former appears in the late sixth century and lasts for scarcely fifty years; the latter is confined to the sixth century. The psykters referred to in inscriptions and literature were evidently of metal, and some are so described (e.g. Nikostratos in Athenaios VI. 230 d; Phylarchos in Athenaios IV. 142 d; Kallixeinos in Athenaios 199 d–200 a; I.G., II–III², 1542, 22).

KALATHOS (Greek κάλαθος). A kind of krater with slightly flaring sides and a spout on one side near the base. Fig. 90.

[9] Cf. Viedebantt in Pauly-Wissowa, Real-Encyclopädie, s.v. kotyle, col. 1547.

[10] The word used, πυθμήν, occurs as meaning both the foot and the bottom of a vase; cf. Athenaios XI. 488 f.

The Greek word κάλαθος means wool basket (Aristophanes *Lysistrata* 579; Hesychios), also a cup (Martial VIII.6. 15 f.; Hesychios), and a psykter (Hesychios). The shape of the Greek wool basket is well known from repre-sentations on vases (see illustration on p. 17) and is described by Pliny (*N.H.* XXI.23) as widening gradually from a narrow base. Since the vase illustrated in fig. 90 and a number of cups (cf. fig. 188) are of this general shape the name kalathos has been applied to them for convenience. That the vase in fig. 90 was used for wine is suggested by the scenes depicted on it— Alkaios and Sappho on one side, Dionysos and a nymph on the other. The spout would be stopped up until the wine was drawn. The shape is rare.

LEKYTHOS (Greek λήκυθος, ληκύθιον). One-handled jug with narrow neck and deep mouth. Used for oil and unguents and as an offering for the dead. Figs. 91–102.

To judge from the evidence, the Greek word lekythos was used in Athens to signify (1) the athlete's oil bottle, that is, the vase now generally called aryballos (cf. p. 16), (2) the form illustrated in figs. 91–102, also probably (3) as a generic term for oil jug.

(1) That lekythos means the athlete's oil bottle is shown by the following quotations and inscription: "A lekythos and brassière! a strange conjunc-tion. How comes the sword beside a looking-glass? What art thou, man or woman?" (Aristophanes *Thesmophoriazousai* 139 ff.[11]); "he lost his leky-thion" (in the famous passage in Aristophanes' *Frogs* 1198 ff., where it must refer to something constantly carried, like the athlete's oil bottle); "the leky-thos ('legythos') belongs to Asopodoros" on a kind of aryballos from Athens signed by Douris (cf. fig. 106; Beazley, *B.S.A.*, 1927–1928, vol. XXIX, pp. 187, 205 f., and *Archäologischer Anzeiger*, 1928, col. 571).

(2) That the word was also used for the shape illustrated in figs. 91 ff. is shown by the fact that vases of this form frequently occur on vase paintings as offerings to the dead (see illustrations on pp. 15, 18); for the Scholiast on Plato (*Hippias Minor* 368 c) tells us that the Athenians called lekythos a vessel in which they brought unguents to the dead, and Aristophanes (*Ekklesiazousai* 996) refers to someone as "the man who paints lekythoi for the dead."

(3) That, however, the word was also used generically for any kind of oil jug is indicated by the following evidence:

According to the Scholiast on Aristophanes' *Ploutos* 810, lekythos is a name given to vessels used for oil (τὰ ἐλαιοδόχα ἀγγεῖα). In a cooking scene in Aristophanes' *Birds* 1589, a slave exclaims, "There is no oil in the lekythos"; in a description of household stores in Aristophanes' *Ploutos*

[11] Tr. Rogers, except for the opening phrase.

810 f., Karion says, "The lekythoi are full of perfume." A vase of the shape illustrated in fig. 95 is used with a funnel in an oil-selling scene (Waldhauer, *Archäologischer Anzeiger*, 1927, p. 74, fig. 2). On a proto-Corinthian "lekythos" from Cumae in the British Museum (A 1054) is the inscription: "I am the lekythos ('leqythos') of Tataie; whoever steals me shall become blind" (*Monumenti antichi . . . dei Lincei*, vol. XXII, pl. 51,1, col. 308); on an

Riezler, *Weissgrundige attische Lekythen*, pl. 23

Woman bringing wreaths in a basket to place on a gravestone. On the steps are lekythoi and oinochoai. Behind the monument appears the mound over the grave. From a lekythos in the National Museum, Athens, no. 1935 (CC. 1692). About 450

Apulian lekythos from Eboli, "The lekythos ('lachythos') belongs to Dionysios, the son of Matalos" (*Annali dell' Inst. di corr. arch.*, 1831, pl. D, 1–2).

The word lekythos had evidently a wide meaning. Archaeologists, however, confine it to the shape illustrated in figs. 91–102.

There are three principal types of lekythos:

Type I. Continuous curve from neck to base (cf. figs. 91, 92). This was the characteristic form during the first half of the sixth century.

Type II. Shoulder set off from body (cf. figs. 93–98). The form begins about the middle of the sixth century and is common throughout the fifth.

Type III. Squat body, broad at base and with no distinct shoulder (cf. figs. 99–102). The form is popular during the second half of the fifth century and the fourth. Scenes in women's apartments are frequent on examples of this type, indicating that such jugs were commonly used by women.

ARYBALLOS (Greek ἀρύβαλλος). Oil bottle with narrow neck, commonly used by athletes at the bath. Figs. 103–108.

The word ἀρύβαλλος occurs only twice in Attic[12]: (1) for a draw purse (Antiphanes in Pollux X.152), (2) for a vase from which Athena pours ambrosia on the head of Demos (Aristophanes *Knights* 1094). In the latter passage it is used in a hexameter line, and evidently to jingle with ἀρύταινα (cf. Beazley, *B.S.A.*, 1927–1928, vol. XXIX, p. 194); it is therefore not necessarily Attic usage. Athenaios (XI.783 f.) defines aryballos as a cup and Pollux (X.63; cf. VII.166) as a bath implement, but both quote the passage in the *Knights* as their authority, so they do not amplify the evidence. On the other hand aryballis is defined by Hesychios as a Dorian word for lekythos (cf. also *s.v.* ἀρβύνδα); and aryballos is said to occur in Dorian writers (Bekker's *Anecdota* 444, 23). It seems likely from this evidence that aryballos was a Dorian name for the shape illustrated in figs. 103–106; the Attic name was lekythos or lekythion (cf. p. 14).

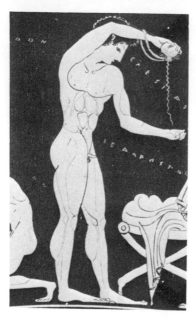

Furtwängler and Reichhold,
Griechische Vasenmalerei, pl. 157

From a scene in the gymnasium: a youth pouring oil into his hand from an aryballos preparatory to rubbing his body with the liquid. The oil bottle (part of the mouth restored) is attached to his wrist by a cord. From a calyx krater in the Staatliche Museen, Berlin, no. 2180. About 510–500

The shape is often represented in vase paintings and on tombstones as suspended from the wrist of an athlete (see illustration at left), or hanging on the wall together with a strigil and sponge, or occasionally as used by women at the bath (cf. Beazley, *B.S.A.*, 1927–1928, vol. XXIX, p. 187, note 5). It is curious, however, that not many actual Athenian examples in terracotta have been found, though Corinthian ones are exceedingly numerous.

There are two chief types of aryballos:

TYPE I. "Corinthian." Round body and broad disk-shaped mouth; generally one handle (cf. fig. 103). This form, so common in Corinth, appears to have had only a short vogue in Attica. It appears in vase representations from about 550 to 520, and a few actual examples of that period exist.

TYPE II. "Attic." Hemispherical mouth and generally two narrow handles with projections (cf. figs. 104–106).

[12] Possibly also in Theopompos Frag. 85, Kock.

ALABASTRON (Greek ἀλάβαστος, the earlier Attic form, or ἀλάβασ-τρον). Elongated, narrow-necked vase for holding perfumes. It has no handles but sometimes has string holes or ears. Figs. 109-111.

Krates (in Athenaios VI. 268 a) in describing a Utopian bathroom speaks of an alabastos of perfume coming to one of its own accord as soon as needed. Suidas (s.v. λήκυθον) says that "the Athenians call a perfume lekythos an alabastron" and defines the alabastron as "a vessel for perfume without handles" (μὴ ἔχον λαβάς). Pliny (N.H. IX.113) compares the pear-shaped pearl, rounded at the bottom and narrow at the top, with an alabastrum.

Furtwängler and Reichhold, *Griechische Vasenmalerei*, pl. 57, 1

Helen sits by her wool basket making roves; Klytaimestra is bringing an alabastron, holding it carefully upright, for it is full. A mirror hangs on the wall. From a pyxis in the British Museum, no. E 773. About 460

Vases of the shape illustrated in figs. 109–111 are represented in vase paintings of women at their toilet and bringing offerings to the dead (see illustrations on pp. 17, 21). Actual examples of alabastra have been found in different materials, especially glass, terracotta, and alabaster, which derives its name from the vase. The name is probably of Egyptian origin — perhaps derived from * ʿa-la-baste, "vase of Ebaste," goddess of the city Bubastos in Egypt (cf. Sethe, *Sitzungsberichte der Preuss. Akad. der Wissenschaften*, 1933, pp. 887–889).

On this evidence the name alabastron has been convincingly applied to the shape.

The form appears throughout the sixth and fifth centuries with little change.

ASKOS (Greek ἀσκός, wineskin). Vase with circular body, convex top, and arched handle meeting the spout. Figs. 112, 113.

The name has been applied to this shape of vase because of a fancied re-semblance to a wineskin, but without justification. The shape is well adapted for pouring oil, the liquid coming out in drops or a thin stream, as experiments show; it is even better for this use than the lekythos, for the body forms an angle with the spout.

The extant examples range in date from the early fifth into the fourth century.

Besides the canonical shape a number of variations occur (cf. Beazley, A. I. A., 1921, vol. XXV, p. 326).

Riezler, *Weissgrundige attische Lekythen*, pl. 20

Offerings to the dead. On the gravestone are a lyre and a chest; on its steps three lekythoi, an oinochoe, and a marble pyxis. From a lekythos in the Staatliche Museen, Berlin, no. 3262. About 450–440

OINOCHOE (Greek οἰνοχόη, from οἶνος, wine, and χέω, pour). Jug for ladling and pouring wine. Figs. 114–134.

The chorus in Euripides' *Troades* 820 ff. describes Ganymede as filling the kylikes of Zeus with golden oinochoai. Hesychios defines the oinochoe as a vessel for pouring; the *Etymologicum Gudianum* as a ladle (τὸ κύαθον). Phrynichos (*Praeparatio sophistica*) describes it as a vessel from which the wine was poured into the cups and adds that it resembled a little pitcher.

In vase paintings this shape commonly occurs both for ladling the wine from the krater and for pouring it into the wine cup (see illustrations on pp. 7, 19, 24). Jugs of this shape also appear with lekythoi as offerings on tombs (see illustrations on pp. 15, 18).

On this evidence the name oinochoe has been applied to the shape.

The oinochoe is one of the commonest of Greek vases and a great variety of forms exists. The mouth is trefoil or round; the body is slender or bulbous; the neck and shoulder are either set off from, or form a continuous curve with, the body; the handle is high or low. The slender type with continuous curve has sometimes been called olpe (Greek ὄλπη) by archaeologists; but this distinction is not borne out by ancient writers, who use olpe (and olpis) as a wine jug or oil jug without describing the shape. Apparently neither ὄλπη nor ὄλπις is an Attic word. The bulbous type with trefoil mouth and low foot was used particularly during the Attic festival of the Choes for the wine drunk in competition, each participant using his own jug (cf. Deub-

Athena pouring a drink for Herakles. The trefoil-shaped mouth of the oinochoe can be plainly seen. From a kylix in the Museum antiker Kleinkunst, Munich, no. 2648.
About 490

ner, *Attische Feste*, p. 97). Diminutive examples of this type with childhood scenes have often been found in children's graves and were apparently given to children as presents during the Choes festival (cf. Deubner, *op. cit.*, pp. 114 ff.).

The principal types of oinochoe are:

TYPE I. Slender body with continuous curve from mouth to base (cf. figs. 114–116). This form is common in black-figure but occurs rarely in red-figure.

TYPE II. Slender body with shoulder slightly set off from body (cf. fig. 117). The form occurs in both black-figure and red-figure.

TYPE III. Bulbous body with continuous curve from mouth to base, trefoil

19

mouth and low foot, low handle (cf. figs. 118–121). In the later fifth and fourth century this shape is common in diminutive examples.

TYPE IV. Bulbous body with offset neck and round mouth (cf. figs. 122, 123).

TYPE V. Bulbous body with offset neck and trefoil mouth (cf. figs. 124–126).

In addition to these five types there are a number of other, variant forms (cf. figs. 127–134; for the shape shown in Pfuhl, *Malerei und Zeichnung der Griechen*, vol. III, fig. 787, cf. Messerschmidt, *Röm. Mitt.*, 1932, vol. XLVII, p. 127).

PYXIS (Greek πυξίς). Round box for holding cosmetics and toilet articles. Figs. 135–145.

To judge from the literary evidence given below, the word pyxis, though used for toilet box in Roman times, was not the Attic name of this shape in the classical period. It has, however, been kept for convenience. The Attic name was apparently κυλιχνίς.[13]

The word πυξίς occurs (1) as a box made of boxwood (πύξος) which was used by physicians for their drugs (*Etymologicum magnum, s.v.* πυξίς; cf. Josephus *Bellum Judaicum* 1.30.7); (2) as a little tablet (Suidas, πυξίς· τὸ πινακίδιον) ; (3) as a box made of any material (*Etymologicum magnum, s.v.* πυξίς; Quintilian VIII.6.35); (4) as a container for women's toilet articles. Lucian (*Erotes* 39) describes "a host of pyxides . . . with such treasures as materials for cleaning teeth and aids for darkening eyelids." Martial (*Epigrams* IX.37) gives a picture of an old courtesan "stored away in a hundred pyxides," her teeth, hair, eyebrows, etc., laid aside (cf. also Petronius *Satyricon* 110).

Terracotta boxes of the shape in question have been found containing rouge, cosmetics, etc. (cf. Langlotz, *Griechische Vasen . . . der Universität Würzburg*, no. 683; Brueckner and Pernice, *Ath. Mitt.*, 1893, vol. XVIII, p. 167), and on them scenes with women are regularly represented (cf. Beazley in Caskey, *Attic Vase Paintings in . . . Boston*, p. 35). Moreover, boxes of this shape occur in scenes of women's apartments on both vases and grave reliefs (see illustration on p. 10). There is therefore no doubt that they were used by women for their toilet.

The pyxis was especially popular from the middle of the fifth century on. The shape occurs also in marble, with painted decorations and often with a high knob; it is so represented on vases, generally in scenes of offerings to the dead (see illustration on p. 18; also illustration on p. 10).

There are several types of pyxis:

TYPE I. Bowl-shaped body and three broad feet (cf. fig. 135). This shape is confined to the sixth century.

[13] Cf. M. J. Milne in a forthcoming article in the *A J.A.*

Type II. Low, concave sides; dome-shaped lid; low foot (cf. fig. 136). This shape was popular in the late fifth and fourth century.

Type III. High, concave sides; cover with handle (cf. figs. 137–142).

Type IV. Cylindrical, with flat lid and no handle (cf. figs. 143–145).

PLEMOCHOE (Greek πλημοχόη, from πλήμη, brimming over, and χέω, pour). Vase with turned-in rim, high foot, and lid. Figs. 146–148.

Sudhoff, *Aus dem antiken Badewesen*, p. 55, fig. 42

Women bathing. In the center three women at a washbasin; on either side an attendant, one with an alabastron, the other with a plemochoe. From a vase now lost. About 470–460

Athenaios (XI.496 a, b) defines the plemochoe as "a terracotta vessel shaped like a top standing on a steady foot." Kritias (in Athenaios, *loc. cit.;* cf. Wilamowitz, *Analecta Euripidea*, pp. 162 ff.) speaks of pouring plemo-choai "with words of good omen into the chasm of earth" (εἰς χθόνιον χάσμα; where χθόνιον perhaps suggests the dead[14]). Athenaios (*loc. cit.*) also informs us that it was used during the Eleusinian mysteries when, on the last day "they filled two plemochoai and set them up one to the east, one to the west, and then overturned them, saying mystic words as they did so."

These descriptions apply fairly well to the shape illustrated in figs. 146–148. The vase may well be likened to a top on a firm foot. It is frequently represented in vase paintings, especially of the middle and second half of the fifth century, when it occurs among the offerings brought by Athenian women to the graves, often in conjunction with the alabastron; also in scenes

---

[14] The action of the *Peirithous*, from which this fragment comes, takes place in the Underworld. For a con-jecture, based on the word plemochoai, that the chorus consisted of Eleusinian mystai, cf. Wilamowitz, *loc. cit.*

of women at their toilet (for instance, at the bath; see illustration on p. 21), receiving gifts, and engaging in religious ceremonies (Daremberg and Saglio, *Dictionnaire, s.v.* dios Kodion, p. 265, fig. 2450, but see correction by Beazley, *Greek Vases in Poland*, pp. 40 f.; Bulas, *C. V.: Pologne—Goluchow: Musée Czartoryski*, pl. 32, 3).

Important for the determination of the use of the vase is the deeply turned-in rim, evidently intended to prevent a liquid from spilling (Robinson, *Annual Report of the Museum of Fine Arts, . . . 1899*, p. 76). Experiments show that a liquid can be conveniently carried in it, the rounded upper side and deep rim holding back the fluid as it swashes to and fro; also that the liquid can be easily poured out from the vase, when full, up to a certain point, after which it becomes exceedingly difficult. (Here we may remember the derivation of plemochoe.) We know that perfume and oil were two toilet necessities commonly used in bathing and that perfume was used in religious ceremonies (*I.G.*, V, 2, 514, 17; Dittenberger, *Sylloge*[3], 999; cf. Eitrem, *Opferritus und Voropfer der Griechen und Römer*, pp. 82 f.); also that the Greeks brought wine, milk, oil, water, and perfume to the dead (Plutarch *Aristeides* XXI.3; Aischylos *Persians* 613 ff.); and that in Athenian grave rites both "washing water" (ἀπόνιμμα) and perfume were offered at the tomb (Kleidemos in Athenaios IX.410 a).

From this evidence it seems reasonable to suppose that the shape was used for containing perfume both for personal use and for religious rites, especially at the grave. Perhaps it was the perfume vase regularly used after the bath, and was for this reason used also in grave rites and purifications, both of which may have been regarded as ritual baths. The perfume was presumably diluted or of a cheap variety used in large quantities, since a vase of this shape would hold a good deal (cf. the cheap perfume carried in a goat's skin, Dittenberger, *Orientis Graeci inscriptiones selectae*, 629, 35–47). It seems also possible, though by no means certain, that the vase was the Greek plemochoe, though the word as it occurs in literature seems rather too specialized for this not uncommon vase. The other names proposed for this shape by archaeologists—kothon (a soldier's drinking cup), and smegmatotheke—are even less convincing.

Terracotta examples of various types have been found in graves dated about 540–500 at Rhitsona (cf. Burrows and Ure, *J.H.S.*, 1911, vol. XXXI, p. 79, and *B.S.A.*, 1907–1908, vol. XIV, pp. 268, 274, 305 ff.); but the same general form must have lasted for some time, for representations of it frequently occur on vases dating from the second half of the fifth century, unless these are intended for marble examples (cf. Caskey, *Attic Vase Paintings . . . . in Boston*, p. 49, fig. 35).

LEKANIS (Greek λεκανίς). A flat dish with cover and with two handles set horizontally. Fig. 149.

The word λεκάνη (and its derivatives λεκανίσκη, λεκάνιον, λεκανίδιον, etc.) was widely used to signify flattish bowls employed for different purposes—to hold food, for washing, to vomit into, etc. (cf. Ure, *Met. Mus. Studies*, 1932, vol. IV, p. 18). The word lekanis, on the other hand, apparently signifies a bowl used for a special purpose; Photios defines it as a terracotta dish or flat bowl (κεραμέα λοπάς· καὶ τὰ ἐκπέταλα τρύβλια), and adds the important information that "the ancients called podanipter (foot bath) what we call the lekane, whereas they called lekanion and lekanis vessels with handles (lit. ears, ὦτα) for cooked food (ὄψον) and the like."

Jahrbuch des deutschen archäologischen Instituts, 1900, vol. XV, pl. 2

Friends bringing gifts to a bride—lebetes gamikoi, a loutrophoros, a lekanis, a chest, and a wool basket. From a pyxis in the Staatliche Museen, Berlin, no. 3373. Fourth century

He also says that at the Epaulia (the day after the wedding) "fathers sent gifts to the brides—jewelry in boxes and girls' playthings in lekanides." Elsewhere (*s.v.* κέραμον) he says that brides brought them into their bridegrooms' houses, and that spices and warp threads were placed in them. Hesychios defines lekanides as "terracotta dishes and dishes in which they brought ἔνθρυπτα (cakes in wine? ἀνθρυπτὰ MS.) to the newly married." Lucian (*Erotes* 39) in describing women prinking lists silver lekanides among their toilet vases.

Representations on vases of the shape illustrated in fig. 149 are regularly taken from the life of women. Moreover, in a scene on a red-figured pyxis, among the wedding gifts being brought to the bride this shape is included (see illustration on this page).

On this evidence Deubner (*Jahrbuch des deutsch. arch. Inst.*, 1900, vol. XV, p. 152) has plausibly identified the shape as the lekanis. On the other hand, the use of the word by Pollux in VI.110 suggests a bowl without a cover. The identification can, therefore, not be regarded as certain.

23

The form appears from the early sixth century on; it is especially popular during the second half of the fifth century. The substantial handles have attachments imitating metal technique. Serving as a handle to the lid is a cylindrical stem terminating in a disklike knob of which the upper side is recessed and has a central depression; the foot is spreading (cf. fig. 149).

OTHER COVERED BOWLS. The shape is similar to that of the lekanis, but instead of two handles there is only one (without attachments) or none, the disklike knob has no recess or depression on the upper side, and the foot is torus-shaped instead of spreading (cf. figs. 150, 151).

Furtwängler and Reichhold, *Griechische Vasenmalerei*, pl. 61

Youths making merry. One is pouring wine into another's cup; a third is bringing a fresh supply in a garlanded amphora. From a volute krater in Arezzo. About 510

KYLIX (Greek χύλιξ). Two-handled cup with comparatively shallow bowl and generally with a high foot. Figs. 152–166.

The word χύλιξ was commonly applied to a drinking cup: "They were drawing full kylikes of wine" (Pherekrates 108.30, Kock); "a kylix of wine mixed half and half with water" (Aristophanes *Ploutos* 1132). In referring to a feast Pindar (in Athenaios XI.480 c) mentions Athenian kylikes. Athenaios (XI.470 e, 478 e) describes the kylix as having handles.

Several inscriptions on actual examples of the shape illustrated in figs. 152–166 contain the word kylix. On the rim of an Attic black-glazed specimen in Odessa is the inscription: "I am a kylix with a pleasant drink dear to him who drinks the wine" (von Stern, *Philologus*, 1913, vol. LXXII, p. 547). On the foot of a late black-figured example in the British Museum (B 450) is incised: "I am the decorated kylix of lovely Philto" (*J.H.S.*, 1885, vol. VI, p. 373; *I.G.*, XII.1, 719). On a cup found in Athens, now lost but described as a poculum rotundum in *C.I.G.*, I, 545, was an inscription: "The kylix belongs to Kephisophon; if anyone breaks it he shall pay a drachma; it is a gift from Xeny . . . ."[15] Furthermore, on Athenian vases banqueters are often shown drinking from cups of this shape (see illustration on p. 24); sometimes the guests are represented playing kottabos, with a finger crooked through one handle to throw the wine left in the bottom at a mark.

On this convincing evidence the name kylix has been applied to the shape.

The kylix was specially popular at the end of the sixth and the beginning of the fifth century. The strongly spreading bowl, sometimes more than fifteen inches in diameter, represents a distinct achievement in pottery, and the difficulty of decorating such a surface invited the best efforts of contemporary vase painters.

There are several types of kylix:

Type I. Lip and foot set off from bowl (cf. figs. 152–158).

Type II. Lip forms continuous curve with bowl; foot offset (cf. figs. 159–162).

Type III. Lip, bowl, and stem form continuous curve (cf. figs. 163–166).

KANTHAROS (Greek κάνθαρος). Two-handled cup with deep bowl and generally with a high foot. Figs. 167–169.

The word κάνθαρος means dung beetle; it was also applied to a cup. Some archaeologists have seen a resemblance between the beetle and the shape illustrated in figs. 167–169 and have explained the derivation accordingly, but this seems far-fetched; so too does the derivation from the fancied similarity between the cup and the harbor of the Peiraieus named κανθάρου λιμήν. Philetairos (in Athenaios XI.474 d, e) derives the name from a potter Kantharos.[16]

Athenaios (XI.473 d) lists the kantharos among the drinking cups and describes it (XI.488 f) as resting on "a thin-stemmed, broad-based foot" (ἀπὸ ἰξέος ἀρχόμενον καταλήγοντα δ' εἰς πλατύτερον). From Macrobius (*Saturnalia* V.21.16) we learn that it was especially associated with Dionysos (Liberi patris cantharus). Dionysos in representations on vases and in sculpture often holds a cup of this shape (see illustration on p. 26).

On this evidence the name kantharos has been applied to the shape illustrated in figs. 167–169. It must be remembered, however, that the kotylos is also associated with Dionysos (cf. p. 27) by Pamphilos (in Athenaios

[15] The inscription on a fourth example (Athens, National Museum 12847) which has been read as "beautiful phiale," φειάλα καλά (Nicole, *Catalogue des vases peints du Musée national d'Athènes*, supplement, p. 175), is really "Phetala (the name of a girl) is beautiful" (Wolters, *Ath. Mitt.*, 1913, vol. XXXVIII, pp. 199 f.).

[16] An obscure passage; perhaps a pun is intended.

XI.478 c). And a vase of the "kantharos" shape from Thespiai in the Louvre is called kotylos in the verse inscribed on it: "Mogea presents as a gift to his wife Eucharis, the daughter of Eutretiphantos, a kotylos that she may drink her fill" (cf. Pottier in Daremberg and Saglio, *Dictionnaire*, *s.v.* cotyla, p. 1550; *I.G.*, VII, 3467). The most reasonable explanation of this apparent contradiction is that kotylos (or kotyle) was a generic term for cup (cf. pp. 27 f.). So the Greek cup called kantharos may well have been the shape here discussed.

Dionysos with a kantharos. From a column krater
in the Metropolitan Museum. About 500

The shape is not common in Athenian pottery, though many representations of it occur in vase paintings. Probably metal was the usual material, for the high curving handles are not well adapted to ceramics. Besides the forms illustrated in figs. 167-169, kantharoi in the shape of human heads sometimes occur.

SKYPHOS (Greek σκύφος). Also called kotyle, see below. Deep cup with low foot (or none) and two handles. Figs. 170-177.

Hesychios defines the σκύφος as a cup (εἶδος ποτηρίου, ἢ ἔκπωμα). Euripides (*Cyclops* 390 f.) describes the Cyclops' skyphos as three cubits wide and four cubits deep. We are told that the skyphos was used by country people (Alkman and Asklepiades of Myrlea in Athenaios XI. 498 f–499 a), but it was also sometimes made of silver or gold ("Hesiod" in Athenaios XI. 498 b and Aischylos in Athenaios XI. 499 a). It could have handles (Simonides in Athenaios XI. 498 e: οὐατόεντα σκύφον), ·was popular with the Boeotians (Athenaios XI. 500 a), and was commonly used by Herakles (Macrobius *Saturnalia* V. 21. 16: scyphus Herculis poculum est). Athenaios (XI. 500 a) speaks of "Heraclean knots" on handles of skyphoi.

Since the shape in question was one popular in Boeotia (especially for the Kabeiric vases); since it is represented, at least in later monuments, as held by Herakles (Zoega, *Li Bassirilievi antichi di Roma*, pls. LXX, LXXII); and·

since it was sometimes fashioned with knotted handles (cf. Daremberg and Saglio, *Dictionnaire, s.v.* scyphus, p. 1160, fig. 6251) it is possible that skyphos is the proper name to apply to it.

Cups of the shape illustrated in figs. 170–177 appear in the hands of revelers in vase paintings (see illustrations on pp. 24, 27).

The shape is often called kotyle by archaeologists. The following evidence, however, shows that the Greek κοτύλη (κότυλος, κοτυλίσκος) was probably a generic term for a cup. Apollodoros (in Athenaios XI. 479 a) says that "the ancients called

Furtwängler and Reichhold, *Griechische Vasenmalerei*, pl. 61

Man drinking from a skyphos to the music of the flute. From a volute krater in Arezzo. About 510

anything hollow κοτύλη"; medical writers use the word κοτύλη to signify the socket of a joint. In the proverb, "There is many a slip 'twixt the cup and the lip," the Greek word for cup is kotyle (Athenaios XI. 478 e). Kotyle and kotylos seem to refer to no fixed shape, for they are described by Athenaios, quoting various authorities, as one-handled (XI.478 b, f), having no handles (XI.478 e), sometimes having a handle (XI.478 b), resembling a deep washbasin (XI.478 b, e), high and hollow (XI.479 a), resembling a krater (krateriskos; XI.479 c), belonging specially to Dionysos (XI. 478 c), used for libations (XI.478 c), and for ladling (XI.482 a; cf. also Pollux VI. 19). The word kotyle occurs also as a dry or liquid measure[17]: "They (the Athenians) were oppressed by both hunger and thirst—the Syracusans having for eight months given them each only a kotyle of water and two kotylai of bread a day" (Thucydides VII. 87.2).

[17] Cf. Viedebantt in Pauly-Wissowa, *Real-Encyclopädie*, vol. XI, cols. 1546 ff.

Three actual vases are called kotylos in inscriptions. A one-handled cup from Kythera in the British Museum (F 595) is inscribed ἡμικοτύλιον, "half-kotyle," evidently a measure (Rolfe, *Harvard Studies in Classical Philology*, 1891, vol. II, p. 98; *I.G.*, V.1,945); a two-handled one from Boeotia has the inscription: "I am the kotylos of Gorginos, the beautiful cup of a beautiful owner" (Rolfe, *op. cit.*, pp. 89 ff.), here, it would seem, referring to the actual cup. A vase of the "kantharos" shape is called kotylos in the verse inscribed on it (cf. p. 26).

From this miscellaneous and contradictory evidence it seems impossible to identify the kotyle with a specific shape.

Double rhyton on a coin of Arsinoe II, Philadelphos; struck by Ptolemy II or III. Third century

There are two chief types of skyphos:

TYPE I. Upward-curving handles placed below lip (cf. figs. 170–173).

TYPE II. Handles set horizontally, level or almost level with rim; torus foot (cf. figs. 174, 176, 177). Sometimes one handle is horizontal, the other vertical (cf. fig. 175).

RHYTON (Greek ῥυτόν). Drinking horn in the form of an animal's head and curved like a horn. Figs. 178–180.

Hedylos, of the first half of the third century B.C. (in Athenaios XI. 497 b-e), refers to the double horn of Arsinoe as a rhyton. Since a double horn is represented on coins of Arsinoe (see illustration above) it is certain that this general shape was called rhyton at that period. Dorotheos, of the early Roman Empire (in Athenaios XI. 497 e), compares rhyta to horns, derives the name from ῥύσις, "stream," and says that people drank the liquid through the hole at the bottom. Epinikos, who lived about 200 B.C. (in Athenaios XI. 497 a, b), describes rhyta as cups in the form of animals, groups, etc. Astydamas, probably the fourth-century poet of that name (in Athenaios XI. 496 e), mentions rheonta (ῥέοντα) in the forms of a griffin and a Pegasos. Philoxenos of Leukas (fourth century B.C.) speaks of drinking from προτομαί and κέρατα, "fore parts of animals and horns" (Frag. d, Diehl).[18]

Horn-shaped cups often appear in the hands of banqueters in Athenian vase paintings; and on some Apulian vases cups in the form of animals' heads are actually in use at banquets (Panofka, *Die griechischen Trinkhörner*, pls. I, III).

[18] Cf. C. I. G., 2852, 39 ff.; Homolle, B. C. H., 1882, vol. VI, pp. 115 f., where the word προτομή also occurs.

From this evidence we know that rhyton, rheon, and protome were names applied to horn-shaped vases in the form of animals during the fourth century and later. Rhyton and rheon, it would seem, were limited to those which had a hole in the bottom (cf. the use of ῥεῖν in inventories to describe leaky vessels, *I.G.*, II–III², 1443, 132; 1444, 1–4, 22; 1640, 21). Whether any one of these names was in use during the period of our ceramic examples is not known.

Girl with ladle filling her master's phiale for the libation.
From a kylix in the British Museum, E 65. About 480

PHIALE (Greek φιάλη). Shallow bowl without handles and generally with a central boss. Used for drinking and pouring libations. Fig. 181.

References made to the phiale by Greek writers indicate its uses. "Let him distribute in the silver phialai the strong child of the vine" (Pindar *Nemean* IX. 51 f.). "Let them carry the phialai on the tips of their fingers, bringing them carefully to the banquet guests" (Pollux VI. 95). "He who stood last of them, Psammetichos, had no phiale; so taking off his helmet he held it out and poured the libation with it" (Herodotos II.151). The phiale is sometimes referred to as "with a central boss," μεσόμφαλος (Ion and Theopompos Com. in Athenaios XI. 501 f–502 a; Pollux VI. 98). Aristotle compares it to a shield (*Rhetoric* III.4. 4 and *Poetics* 21. 6, 8, from Timotheos Frag. 22, Wilamowitz), and the two words ἀσπίς and φιάλη are used interchangeably in Pausanias V.10.4.

A silver bowl of this shape from Cyprus has incised on it in Cypriote script: "I am the phiale of Epioros" (Wolters, *Ath. Mitt.*, 1913, vol. XXXVIII, pp. 195 f.; Myres, *Handbook of the Cesnola Coll. of Antiquities from Cyprus*, no. 4552). The word Phi (ala) is inscribed on a bowl with the bust of Alexandreia from Boscoreale (*Monuments et mémoires . . . Fondation Eugène Piot.*, vol. V, p. 42). On Athenian vases there are frequent representations of bowls of this shape used for drinking and libations (see illustrations on pp. 8, 29).

From this evidence it seems certain that the shape illustrated in fig. 181 is the Greek phiale.

The shape is rare in terracotta. The many examples represented on Athenian vases were probably of metal, as is indicated by the flutings; there are also frequent references to metal phialai in literature and inscriptions.

MASTOS (Greek μαστός, a breast). Cup in the shape of a woman's breast. Fig. 182.

Athenaios (XI. 487 b) says that "according to Apollodoros of Kyrene the Paphians called a drinking cup a mastos." Hesychios defines the word as a cup. In two inscriptions from Delos and Oropos the mastos is listed in inventories (*I.G.*, XI, 1307, cf. 1308, 2; VII, 3498). Cups in the shape of a woman's breast occasionally occur in pottery. They are evidently the Greek mastos.

KYATHOS (Greek κύαθος). Ladle in the form of a cup with foot and long upward-curving handle. Figs. 183, 184.

Xenophon mentions the kyathos in the *Education of Cyrus* I.3.9 (tr. Miller): "Now it is a well-known fact that the king's cupbearers, when they proffer the phiale, draw off some of it with the kyathos, pour it into their left hand, and swallow it down—so that if they should put poison in they may not profit by it." Hesychios defines it as a drop, a small measure, an implement for drawing liquids (ἀντλητήριον), a little iron egg, and says that it holds two unciae of liquid. Suidas compares it to a spoon (κοχλιάριον). The *Etymologicum Gudianum* describes it as an ἀντλητήριον with a long handle.

These references suggest a spoon-shaped ladle of small capacity such as is preserved in bronze examples (cf. nos. 645, 647, 648, 652 in this Museum) and occurs in representations in Greek vase painting (see illustrations on pp. 8, 13, 29). The deeper shape[19] illustrated in figs. 183 and 184 is adapted for

[19] Athenaios (XI.480 b) defines the kyathis (κυαθίς) as a vessel shaped like a kotyle, evidently referring to a deep receptacle like ours; but since the only passage he quotes is from Sophron the word is apparently not Attic.

dipping and is a ceramic approximation of the bronze form. Moreover the word κυάθεα appears in a graffito on the foot of a stamnos (Hackl, *Münchener archäologische Studien*, [1909], p. 52). As these graffiti on vases presumably refer to potters' orders, the name kyathos was evidently applied also to a terracotta shape. It is therefore not impossible that the shape in question was called kyathos. The known terracotta examples date chiefly from the late sixth and the first half of the fifth century.

Furtwängler and Reichhold, *Griechische Vasenmalerei*, pl. 4

Dining table with food and drink. From an amphora in the Museum antiker Kleinkunst, Munich, no. 2301. About 525

CUPS OF VARIOUS SHAPES. Besides the standard forms, cups of various other shapes sometimes occur (cf. figs. 185–188). An important class is that in which the body is molded in the form of a human head (cf. fig. 187).

STAND. With a flat top on a stemmed foot. Figs. 189, 190.

Only a few such stands have been found. Their use is uncertain. They are not identical with the krater supports (cf. fig. 54), for the latter are hollow and are not flat at the top. In the picture shown above a stand of this form appears to be represented, placed on the table with the food and wine. It is obviously too small to have been a support for the drinking cups. Perhaps it was used for sweetmeats.

PLATE (cf. fig. 191). The usual word for plate or platter was πίναξ. The pinax varied in shape. One with feet and two handles is listed in a fourth-century Attic inscription (*I.G.*, II–III², 120, 44-45). Hippolochos of Mace-

31

don (about 300 B.C.) in Athenaios IV. 130 b mentions a rectangular one. Pollux X. 82 describes pinakes as being round, shallow, or deep. That the pinax could be round seems to be implied also by the use of πινακίσκιον to describe the small disk (πλάστιγξ) at the top of the kottabos stand (Antiphanes in Athenaios XV. 666 f). Hence the name is apparently correctly used for the shape illustrated in fig. 191. On the table shown in the illustration on p. 31, a pinax with food seems to be represented between the little stand and the knife.

In Attic pottery, this shape is common only in the sixth century. The pinakes mentioned in literature and inscriptions are usually of metal (cf. e.g. the passages quoted by Athenaios VI. 229 f–230 e). The word πίναξ means primarily board or plank and must, in the beginning, have been applied to wooden platters.

Fig. 1. H. 22¹¹⁄₁₆ in. Late seventh or early sixth century. Short, broad neck; slightly flaring mouth.

Fig. 2. H. 15¹⁄₁₆ in. First half of sixth century. Neck higher,[1] body broader. flare of mouth accentuated.

Fig. 3. H. 15³⁄₈ in. About 550-540. Neck higher.

Fig. 4. H. 15⁵⁄₁₆ in. Late sixth century. Neck and handles higher, body more elongated, mouth more flaring.

[1] When a comparative is used, "than in the preceding example" is understood.

Fig. 5. Red-figured example. H. 18½ in. About 490. Juncture of sections clearly visible on inside just above lower attachments of handles.

Figs. 6, 7. H. 20⅛ in. About 525. Ridge between body and foot, lower degree of foot slightly higher than upper.

Fig. 8. H. 19⅜ in. About 460. Body less elongated, lower degree of foot consider-ably higher than upper.

Fig. 9. H. 16⁵⁄₁₆ in. Second quarter of sixth century. Ridge between body and foot.

Fig. 10. Boston 98.882. H. 16³⁄₃₂ in. About 490. Echinus foot.

Fig. 11. Würzburg 509. H. 16 in. About 470. Torus foot.

Fig. 12. H. 14⅞₁₆ in. Second quarter of sixth century. Ovoid body, echinus mouth and foot, ridge at juncture of neck and body.

Fig. 13. H. 14¾ in. About 530. Height and width of body about equal, triple handles, ridge between neck and body.

Fig. 14. H. 15⁵₁₆ in. End of sixth century. Body higher than it is wide, triple handles, ridge between neck and body and between body and foot.

Fig. 15. H. 18½ in. About 540. Body wider than it is high, short neck, quadruple handles ending below in attachments imitating metal technique, ridge between neck and body and between body and foot, lid with crowning knob.

Fig. 16. H. 5¾ in. Early fifth century. Elongated body considerably higher than it is wide; triple handles, one entirely, the other partly restored.

Fig. 17. H. 8⅞ in. About 490. Variant of type II a, with straight instead of echinus mouth and double handles.

Fig. 18. H. 12¾ in. About 480. Developed Nolan type. Triple handles. The simple decoration sets off the finely proportioned shape.

Fig. 19. H. 13⅝ in. About 440. Developed Nolan type. Handles with central rib.

Fig. 20. H. 18⅝ in. About 480.
Handles twisted, echinus mouth.

Fig. 21. H. 18⅝ in. About 460.
Handles cylindrical in section,
mouth in two degrees.

Fig. 22. H. 24⅛ in. About 440. Handles
twisted, mouth in two degrees and
slightly higher.

Fig. 23. H. 13¾ in. About 400. Body
forms concave curve at base; mouth in
two degrees and strongly spreading,
handles twisted, lower degree of foot
much higher than upper.

Fig. 24. H. 24½ in. End of sixth century. Prize vase. Mouth and foot echinus-shaped, ridge between neck and body.

Fig. 25 H. 17⁹⁄₁₆ in. About 480–470. No inscription, neck and foot broader.

Fig. 26. Fogg Art Museum 1925. 30.124. H. 31½ in. 340–339. Body more elongated; neck, handles, and foot higher; ogee mouth; spreading foot.

Fig. 27. H. 3⁵⁄₁₆ in. Fourth century. Toy Panathenaic vase.

Fig. 28. Munich 2344. H. 22¹⁄₁₆ in. About 500–490. Mouth of convex outline, foot diminutive and torus-shaped.

Fig. 29. Cabinet des médailles 357. H. 24 in. About 450. Original stand; mouth, handles, and most of neck modern.

Fig. 30. H. 6⁵⁄₁₆ in. About 425. Echinus mouth, narrow neck. Diminutive example used for unguents.

Fig. 31. H. 7³⁄₈ in. Late fifth century. Impressed patterns, mouth lipped, neck narrow, foot in several degrees. Stand modern.

Fig. 32. H. 10½ in. Late sixth century. Long, narrow body; handles double, with attachments imitating metal technique.

Fig. 33. Boston 01.17. H. (with handles) 11¹³⁄₃₂ in. Last quarter of sixth century. High volute handles, torus foot.

Photograph by Giraudon

Fig. 34. Louvre G 2. H. 15³⁄₁₆ in. Last quarter of sixth century. Ribbon handles; foot in two degrees, lower of convex, upper of concave outline; broad ridge between body and foot.

Fig. 35. Gallatin Collection. H. 6³⁄₃₂ in. About 540. Narrow neck, spreading mouth of convex outline, egg-shaped body, torus foot.

Fig. 36. H. 11¼ in. About 480. Mouth convex, handles segmental in section, spreading foot.

Fig. 37. H. 16½ in. About 440. Mouth and handles as in fig. 36, disk foot.

Fig. 38. H. 14¼ in. About 420. Mouth convex, triple handles, disk foot.

Fig. 39. H. 11 in. Middle of fourth century. Mouth lipped, handles with central rib, torus foot in several degrees.

Photograph by Alinari

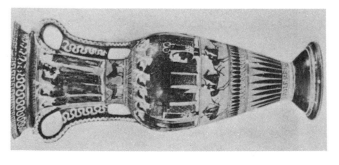

Fig. 42. H. 21⅜ in. Fourth century. Neck and body narrower and more elongated, lip overhanging, high-stemmed foot with spreading base of convex outline.

Fig. 41. Louvre M.N. 558. H. 16⅚ in. Late fifth century. Ridges on neck, foot in two degrees.

Fig. 40. H. 29½ in. About 500. Mouth in three degrees; handles with supports; foot quasi-conical, in several degrees; ridge between neck and body and between body and foot. No bottom, to permit the pouring of libations onto the grave.

Figs. 43, 44. H. 22⅛ in. About 550–540. Wide body, short neck, echinus foot, ridge between body and foot.

Fig. 45. H. 19⅞ in. About 530. Neck higher; body narrower; foot in two degrees, both convex.

Fig. 46. H. 13⅝ in. Late sixth century. Neck still higher, body more elongated. Decoration on mouth no longer extends to handles.

Fig. 47. H. 14⅞ in. About 460. Body forms fuller curve, handles flare out considerably.

Fig. 48. H. 15 in. About 430. Body more elongated, top of mouth convex, lower degree of foot much higher than upper.

Photograph by Alinari

Fig. 49. The François vase, Museo archeologico, Florence. H. (with handles) 26⅜ in. About 570–560. Foot in form of an inverted, flattened echinus. One of the largest vases in existence.

Fig. 50. Boston 90.153. H. (with handles) 30⁷⁄₁₆ in. Last quarter of sixth century. Body more elongated; handles forming compact spirals; mouth with offset lip; foot in two degrees, the lower convex.

Fig. 51. H. (without handles) 25 in. About 450. Body still more elongated, ogee foot.

Fig. 52. Side view of fig. 51.

Fig. 53. H. (with handles) 26⅝ in. About 420. Body higher than it is wide, mouth and foot in several degrees.

Fig. 54. H. on stand (without handles) 23¼ in. About 430. Like fig. 53, but body fluted; vase is set on a hollow stand. Upper parts of handles restored.

CALYX KRATER. See pp. 7–8

Fig. 55. Berlin 2180. H. 13¹³⁄₁₆ in. About 510–500.
Width greater than height; mouth in two degrees, the
upper convex, the lower concave.

Fig. 56. Boston 97.368. H. 17⁷⁄₁₆ in. About 490–480. Width
and height about equal.

Fig. 57. H. 15⅝ in. About 440. Mouth more flaring, curve of handles more accentuated, lower degree of foot higher than upper. Part of ridge between body and foot has fallen off, showing juncture beneath (cf. p. xiii).

Fig. 58. Side view of fig. 57.

Fig. 59. H. 8⁵⁄₁₆ in. End of fifth century. Body more elongated and drawn in at base, overhanging mouth, handles higher.

BELL KRATER. See p. 8

Fig. 60. H. 14⁹⁄₁₆ in. About 450. Mouth in two degrees, the upper convex; disk foot.

Fig. 61. H. 11⅝ in. About 440–430. Curve of body accentuated.

Fig. 62. H. 11³⁄₁₆ in. About 420. Curve of body more accentuated, foot higher and in several degrees.

Fig. 63. H. 15¼ in. Third quarter of fifth century. Lugs instead of loop handles.

Fig. 64. H. 12 in. End of sixth century. Body wider than it is high, mouth in two degrees, disk foot.

Fig. 65. H. 12¾ in. About 460. Steep shoulder; body less squat, narrowing considerably toward base; mouth in three degrees; torus foot.

Fig. 66. H. 14¼ in. About 450. Body more elongated, shoulder less steep, foot in two degrees.

Fig. 67. H. 15 in. About 440. Body still more elongated.

Fig. 68. H. 15¾ in. Early fifth century. Mouth of convex outline, handle at-tachments imitating metal technique. A particularly fine example of the squat type. To obtain so steep a shoulder in a large jar without its sagging is a con-siderable achievement.

Fig. 69. British Museum B 46. H. 13 in. About 560. No neck, low rim of convex outline, steep shoulder.

Fig. 70. Boston 90.154. H.(with stand) 22 in. End of sixth century. Mouth flaring, no neck, high shoulder. Stand strongly articulated, imitating metal technique.

Fig. 71. H. 10½ in. Second half of fifth century. Overhanging mouth in two degrees, short neck, shoulder less steep.

Fig. 72. British Museum B 298. H. 15⅖ in. Late sixth century. Lid preserved.

Fig. 73. H. 22⁵⁄₁₆ in. About 430–420.

Fig. 74. Athens 1659 (CC. 1575). H. 7⅞ in. About 430–420. A variant form with low foot and no neck.

Fig. 75. H. 5 in. About 430–420. Miniature example, probably a toy, complete with lid; left handle restored.

Fig. 76. H. 13¾ in. Second quarter of sixth century. No distinct shoulder, vertical handle reaching to the mouth, inverted echinus foot.

Fig. 77. H. 13⅛ in. Third quarter of sixth century. Handles and moldings imitate metal technique.

Figs. 78, 79. H. 18³⁄₁₆ in. Last quarter of sixth century. Shoulder almost horizontal, body more elongated, disk foot. Attachments of vertical handle imitate metal technique.

Fig. 80. H. 10 in. About 500. Mouth convex, body rather elongated, disk foot.

Fig. 81. Side view of fig. 82.

Fig. 82. H. 14$^{15}\!/_{16}$ in. About 500. Body wider than it is high, with a fine sweep to its curve; mouth convex; disk foot.

Figs. 83, 84. H. 11¾ in. About 460. Height and width of body about equal, over-hanging mouth in several degrees, foot in several degrees.

Fig. 85. H. 16¾ in. About 430. Neck narrower, foot less wide and higher.

Fig. 86. H. 11½ in. About 350. Neck higher, body more elongated, curve of handles accentuated, mouth more flaring.

Fig. 87. Psykter. H. 13⅛ in. About 510. Mouth in two degrees, both of convex outline; torus foot. As only upper and lower parts of stem are preserved, the original height is uncertain.

Fig. 88. Psykter. British Museum E 767. H. 13 in. About 510. Two small loop handles, overhanging mouth, foot in several degrees.

Fig. 89. Psykter. British Museum B 148. H. 12⅗ in. About 550–540. A variant form with double walls and bottom. The wine was poured through the neck; the cooling water, poured through the spout, was later emptied through a hole in the bottom.

Fig. 90. Kalathos. Munich 2416. H. 20⅞ in. About 480–470. Lug handles.

Fig. 91. In the collection of Humfry Payne. H. about 6⅞ in. About 600. Globular body; low neck; deep, convex mouth; wide, spreading foot.

Fig. 92. H. 6⅞ in. Second quarter of sixth century. Egg-shaped body, concave mouth.

Fig. 93. H. 6¾ in. Mid-sixth century. Shoulder slightly offset; short, convex mouth; neck higher; foot smaller.

Fig. 94. H. 6⅛ in. Third quarter of sixth century. Concave shoulder offset sharply from body; spreading, convex mouth; disk foot; ridge between body and foot.

Fig. 95. H. 9⁵⁄₁₆ in. Last quarter of sixth century. Elongated body, spreading foot.

Fig. 96. H. 13⁷⁄₁₆ in. About 480–470. Body almost cylindrical, substantial disk foot, ridge between body and foot.

Fig. 97. H. 11⁷⁄₈ in. About 440. Body slender, almost cylindrical; high neck and handle; deep mouth; thick disk foot.

Fig. 98. H. 10⁷⁄₈ in. End of fifth century. Outline of body forms ogee curve; steep shoulder.

Fig. 99. H. 5⅜ in. About 470. Body higher than it is wide.

Fig. 100. H. 3⅝ in. About 430. Body almost as wide as it is high, short neck, broad foot in two degrees.

Fig. 101. H. 7⅞ in. About 420–410. Neck and mouth higher.

Fig. 102. H. 4¼ in. Early fourth century. Body elongated; mouth forms ogee curve.

Fig. 103. H. 3¹⁄₁₆ in. About 550. Single, broad handle; overhanging mouth; no foot.

Fig. 104. H. 3½ in. Early fifth century. Handles with rectangular projections (right one restored). Stand modern.

Fig. 105. Oxford 1929.175. H. 2⅜ in. About 490-480. Flat bottom, handles with rounded projections.

Fig. 106. Athens 15375. H. 3¹⁵⁄₁₆ in. About
490. One handle, flat bottom.

Fig. 107. H. 4⅝ in. End of sixth
century. Body in form of two female
heads, handles (left one restored)
with rectangular projections.

Fig. 108. H. 2⁷⁄₁₆ in. End of sixth century.
Body in form of three cockleshells, handles
with rectangular projections.

Fig. 109. H. 5 in. End of sixth century. White-ground alabastron, common in this period, perhaps in imitation of alabaster specimens. Stand modern.

Fig. 110. Alabastron. H. 7⅛ in. About 440. Body slenderer, neck higher, mouth thinner. The two small projections imitate string holes but they are not perforated.

Fig. 111. Alabastron. H. 4 in. Early fourth century. Mouth very thin. Stand modern.

Fig. 112. Askos. Oxford 541. H. 2¹³⁄₁₆ in., diam. 3½ in. About 430.

Fig. 113. Askos. H. 2¾ in., l. 6¼ in. About 460. Body in form of a lobster claw.

Fig. 114. Oxford 505. H. (with handle) 12¾ in. Early sixth century. Trefoil mouth, high handle, foot in shape of inverted echinus.

Fig. 115. H. (with handle) 10⁷⁄₁₆ in. Last quarter of sixth century. Round mouth, high handle with attachments on lip.

Fig. 116. H. (with handle) 9¼ in. End of sixth century. Round mouth, high handle with attachments on lip, spreading foot.

Fig. 117. H. 9⅛ in. Fifth century. Overhanging mouth; low, convex foot.

Fig. 118. H. 3¹³⁄₁₆ in. Late sixth century. Handle cylindrical in section, convex foot.

Fig. 119. H. 9⅜ in. About 490-480. Broad central lobe in trefoil mouth, handle with central rib.

Fig. 120. H. 3⅝ in. About 420. Diminutive example (cf. p. 19); flat handle, convex foot.

Fig. 121. H. 9¼ in. Middle of fourth century. Edges of mouth sharp, imitating metalware; handle with central rib; low, echinus foot.

Figs. 122, 123. H. (with handle) 7½ in. Middle of sixth century. High, double handle; the attachments and bosses (for rivets) on inside of mouth imitate metal technique; foot in form of inverted echinus.

Fig. 124. H. 8 9/16 in. Late sixth century. Low handle, disk foot.

Fig. 125. H. (with handle) 16¾ in. About 470–460. High handle with central rib and attachments on lip, disk foot.

Fig. 126. H. 13⅛ in. About 450. Trefoil mouth; low handle with thumb rest on lip; ridge between neck and body: low, convex foot.

Fig. 127. Munich 1828. H. 10¼₆ in. End of sixth century. Beaked spout with disk at each side, neck offset, spreading foot, flanged handle.

Fig. 128. H. (with handle) 8½₆ in. Second half of fifth century. High handle, beaked spout with disk on each side, ogee foot.

Fig. 129. H. (with handle) 8½ in. Third quarter of fifth century. Egg-shaped body, high handle, trefoil mouth, high foot in several degrees.

Fig. 130. H. 5⅜ in. Late fifth or early fourth century. Shoulder sharply set off from body, beaked spout, no foot.

Fig. 131. H. 5¼ in. About 460. Mouth with central lobe, neck offset, flat handle, no foot.

Photograph by Alinari

Fig. 132. Vatican H 530. H. 7⅞ in. About 450. Vertical mouth, neck offset, no foot.

Fig. 133. British Museum 1154. H.(with handle) 10¹³⁄₁₆ in. Second half of fifth century. Shoulder set off from body, mouth in two degrees, torus foot.

Fig. 134. H. (with handle) 6¹⁄₁₆ in. Probably early fifth century. Body in form of a negro's head.

Fig. 135.   Athens 475 (CC. 837). H. 3 9/16 in. End of
sixth century. Knob on lid.

Fig. 136. H. 3 in. Late fifth century. Bronze ring and at-
tachment serve as handle on lid.

Fig. 137. H. 2³⁄₁₆ in. Middle to third quarter of sixth century. Loop handle, no foot.

Fig. 138. H. 4 in. Third quarter of fifth century. Knob handle, torus foot.

Fig. 139. H. 4⅞ in. About 460. Knob handle, high foot.

Fig. 140. H. 4¾ in. Last quarter of fifth century. Handle in form of a knuckle-bone. Wide lid, notches in foot for evaporation in firing and easy handling.

Fig. 141. H. 6¾ in. About 460. Dome-shaped knob, notches in foot.

Fig. 142. H. 1⅞ in. Fifth century Low, notched foot.

Fig. 143. H. 2$\frac{1}{16}$ in. End of sixth century. Torus foot.

Fig. 144. H. 1$\frac{3}{4}$ in. Late fifth century. Rim of lid and foot in several degrees.

Fig. 145. H. 3$\frac{1}{4}$ in. About 420. Rim of lid and foot in several degrees.

Fig. 146. H. 6¾ in. Probably last quarter of sixth century. Deep bowl, flaring foot, turned-in rim extending almost 1½ in. down.

Fig. 147. H. 6³⁄₁₆ in. End of sixth century (?). Bowl shallower; quasi-cylindrical stem resting on low, flaring foot.

Fig. 148. H. 6 in. End of sixth century (?). Ridge at juncture of bowl and foot, turned-in rim extending 1¼ in. down, lid missing.

Fig. 149. H. (with cover) 7 9/16 in. About 420. Knob on
lid in form of disk.

Fig. 150. H. (with cover) 3 1/2 in. Second half of fifth century. One handle.

Fig. 151. H. (with cover) 3 7/8 in. Second half of fifth century. No handle.

Fig. 152. H. 3¾ in., diam. 8¼ in. First quarter of
sixth century. Low, concave mouth; deep bowl; foot
of concave outline.

Fig. 153. H. 5½ in., diam. 10½ in. Second quarter of
sixth century. Lip and foot somewhat higher. So-called
Siana type.

Fig. 154. H. 3¾ in., diam. 5¹¹⁄₁₆ in. Third quarter of
sixth century. So-called Little-Master cup.

Fig. 155. H. 7 in., diam. 11⅛ in. Second quarter of sixth century. High-stemmed foot.

Fig. 156. H. 4⅜ in., diam. 9⅛ in. About 460. Body forms continuous curve with stem; foot offset, ridge between stem and foot.

Fig. 157. H. 3½ in., diam. 8⅞ in. About 460. Ring base, without stem.

Fig. 158. H. (without handles) 3⅝ in., diam. 6⅝ in. Middle of fourth century. Ribbed body with flat bottom and ridge between body and stem; large handles rising higher than lip.

Fig. 159. H. 4¹³⁄₁₆ in., diam. 10 in. About 550. Deep bowl; low, quasi-conical foot; ridge at juncture of bowl and foot.

Fig. 160. H. 4½ in., diam. 8 in. About 550. Bowl slightly shallower, foot higher.

Fig. 161. H. 6¼ in., diam. 15 in. Last quarter of sixth century. Shallow bowl; broad, heavy foot. A form used by the potter Nikosthenes.

Fig. 162. H. 4¼ in., diam. 12⅜ in. About 520. Foot lower and slenderer.

Fig. 163. H. 3⅞ in., diam. 10 in. About 510. Small recess in foot to mark
bottom of stem.

Fig. 164. H. 3⁵⁄₁₆ in., diam. 8⁷⁄₁₆ in. About 480–470. Ridge between stem
and spreading foot.

Fig. 165. British Museum D6. H. 3⅛ in., diam. 5⁵⁄₁₆ in.
About 460. Slender form with wishbone handles.

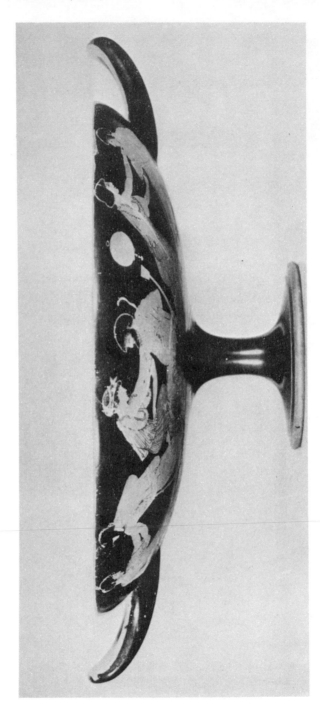

Fig. 166. H. 5⅜ in., diam. 13¼ in. About 490. The beauty of the unbroken curve from the edge of the lip to the bottom of the foot is the result of a century of continued study.

Fig. 167. Boston 95.36. H. (with handles)
$9\frac{1}{2}$ in. About 490–480. High-stemmed foot,
high-curving handles.

Fig. 168. Brussels A 718. H. (with handles) $7\frac{5}{32}$ in.
About 490–480. Mouth and body form continuous
curve; high-curving handles, short-stemmed foot.

Fig. 169. Castle Goluchow 64. H. $4\frac{5}{16}$ in. About
450. Handles do not curve above rim; short-
stemmed foot.

Fig. 170. H. 6⅜ in. About 500. Mouth slightly concave, deep bowl, disk foot of convex outline, ridge between body and foot.

Fig. 171. Boston 76.48. H. 3⁵⁄₁₆ in., diam. 4⅛ in. Early fifth century. Offset, flaring mouth; no foot.

Fig. 172. H. 2⅞ in. About 425. Handles do not curve so sharply upward; bowl not so deep; offset, concave mouth; torus foot.

Fig. 173. H. 3⅛ in. Fifth century. Mouth and bowl form continuous curve; torus foot.

Fig. 174. H. 6½ in. About 460. Torus
foot.

Fig. 175. H. 3¹⁵⁄₁₆ in. About 480. One
handle set horizontally, the other vertically; disk foot.

Fig. 176. H. 3 in. Late fifth century.
Thin walls; bowl narrows sharply toward the base; spreading foot.

Fig. 177. H. 6⅞ in. Middle of fourth
century. Outline of body forms ogee
curve; torus foot.

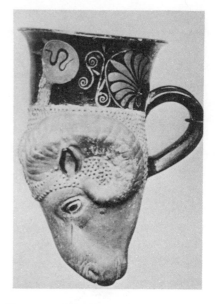

Fig. 178. Boston 03.787. H. 9⅞ in. About 480. Body in form of a mule's head.

Fig. 179. Boston 95.38. H. 8⁵⁄₁₆ in. About 460–450. Body in form of a ram's head.

Fig. 180. H. 5¾ in. About 460. Body in form of a cow's head.

Fig. 181. Phiale. Boston 98.886. H. 1¹³⁄₁₆ in., diam. 6⁷⁄₁₆ in.
About 460. Ribbed bowl imitates metalwork.

Fig. 182. Mastos. British Museum B 375. H. 3⁹⁄₁₀ in.
About 530. One handle set vertically, the other
horizontally.

Fig. 183. Kyathos. H. (with handle)
5¼ in. Late sixth century. Handle with
transverse support; low, flat foot.

Fig. 184. Kyathos. H. (with handle)
5¹¹⁄₁₆ in. Late sixth century. Ridge at
juncture of bowl and disk foot.

Fig. 185. H. 3⁷⁄₁₆ in. End of sixth or early fifth century. No handles; offset, flaring mouth; no foot. Cf. the handleless cups mentioned in an Attic inscription (I.G., II–III², 1640, 22).

Fig. 186. H. 3½ in. End of sixth century. Cup or jug with one handle and no foot. A vase of this general shape in the British Museum is inscribed "half a kotyle," ἡμικοτύλιον, evidently having served as a measure (cf. p. 28).

Fig. 187. H. 7⅜ in. About 490. One handle; body in form of a female head.

Fig. 188. Athens 474 (CC. 637). H. 3 in. Second half of sixth century. Handleless cup of "kalathos" shape (cf. p. 14.)

STAND AND PLATE. See pp. 31–32

Fig. 189. Stand. H. 2¼ in. Middle of
sixth century. Conical stem, flanged rim
and foot.

Fig. 190. Stand. H. 1¹⁵⁄₁₆ in. Second
half of sixth century. Ridge between
top and stem.

Fig. 191. Plate. Boston 00.335. Diam.
6¹¹⁄₁₆ in. End of sixth century. Low
foot. The checker pattern on the rim
effectively frames the decoration.